STATUS OF WOMEN IN RURAL SOCIETIES

Edited By
Dr Ramesh Chaube
Dr Mrs. Kalpana Saini

Distributed by

GYAN

GYAN BOOKS PVT. LTD.
5, Ansari Road, Darya Ganj, New Delhi-110002

aP

ADITYA PUBLISHERS
M.P. - 470113

Status of Women in Rural Societies

ISBN: 81-87725-19-2

Edition 2002
Printed Copies-500

Distributed by
Gyan Books Pvt. Ltd.
5, Ansari Road, Darya Ganj, New Delhi-110002
Phones : 3282060, 3261060, Fax (011) 3285914
E-mail : gyanbook@vsnl.com
Website : http://www.gyanbooks.com

Published by
Aditya Publishers
Jageshwari Mata Complex,
Pathak Ward,
Bina (M.P.) 470113
Phones : (07580) 24372 (O), 23644 (R)

Laser Typesetting at: Sharma Graphic, New Delhi
Printed at: Mehra Offset Press, New Delhi

Contents

Foreword

The organiser of the Seminar. "Status of Women in Rural Societies" held in Department of Anthropology, University of Sagar on 2nd and 3rd Oct, 2001, have done me an honour by asking me to write the foreward to the present proceeding. The proceeding encompasses all those aspects which directly or indirectly are involved in emancipation of rural women.

The value attributed to women's roles by their respective societies in fact, sets the social order of their status. In the absence of socio-cultural renaissance it is difficult to liberate women from putative male domination. The women of rich landowning classes and landless classes of rural societies display remarkable variation. Nonetheless, a general observation can be made that women have always been apparently located in family, supply the necessary labour force and reproduction of human resource. With higher input of political and ideological ingradients and education the rural women can be motivated for upward social mobility, without undermining the traditional values of their respective culture.

I am delighted to note that bulk of the material presented in the seminar cover all such aspects. Majority of the work strives towards economic and political aims which are viewed as inconceivable without altering the status of women in rural India.

By passing new laws opportunities have obviously made it possible for women to use their talents and thus, loosen the bonds of old social mores. The emphasis on social and culture setting, modern education, employment opportunities, family economics, marriage, freedom of movement in the family and outside have strong bearing on the topic under discussion. Thus, to realise the goal the importance of education of girls in rural areas is worth attention. An educated women would ultimately bring her children in an enlightened way and young educated men will not treat their wives in an inferior position at home. Subsequently this will check violence against women, a social phenomenon.

It is true that biological imparative mars the status of women. Her physique and physical form and in view of risk involved for the safety of offspring, she chooses the role of a appeaser. As long as women in rural societies remain under traditional socio-psychological spell their status in the society will cease to improve. The emancipation of rural women, from such odds needs a pragmatic approach.

By virtue of my having long association with the department, it can be construed that right from its inception, the department has made significant contributions and present seminar is one more step in the same direction. I take delight in felicitating the organisers of the seminar.

R.S. Bali

Preface

The status of women in any society depends on a biological fact based on sex-dichotomy. But what is biological and what is cultural in sex differentiation is not established with certainty for all types of activities. It is true that certain physiological functions are sex-linked. Women possess the basic reproductive role which is biologically fixed and this fact creates differentiation statuses of males and females. Thus, traditionally every society, assigns to the males and females different roles and each society expects men and women to behave differently. The division of labour on the basis of sex is found to be present in all societies, modern as well as primitive and according to their roles their status is determined.

The United Nations has defined the status of women as the "conjunction of position of women occupies as a worker, student, mother............of the power and prestige attached to these position, and of the rights and duties she is expected to exercise.

India is a big country and status of women is not uniform in all the rural areas of the country. It varies from place to place and even within the same population living in different ecological cultural settings; factors like, rules of residence, descent, inheritance, marriage, divorce and degree of accultaration, urbanization, modernization and such others may have contributed to this variation. The Constitution of India gives equality of status to Indian women with that of men. However, the question still looms large—whether they have attained the equality in real sense. As we know, there always exists a gap between theory and practice. Therefore, it is not merely equality under law that determines the status of women in a society. Traditions and customs are more powerful and crucial than law in determining women's position within a social structure.

The declaration of International Women's Year by United Nations, during 1975 had attracted the attention of a section of social thinkers and social scientists to examine the women's problem throughout the world.

India is not an exception to that. Since then, a number of anthropologists and sociologists in India have been evaluating the women's position in total gamut of the society. But such studies are mostly confined of the upper and middle class women in urban areas. This is the reason that these has been a gap in our knowledge of women's life in rural societies.

The woman in rural communities plays a more active role as a bread earner of the family, performs hard manual labour, even acts as a more responsible partner and not functioning as a passive human incubator, not confirming herself to hearth and kitchen alone, not parading herself as a beautiful drawing-room showpiece like many of her counterparts, in advanced societies. But in rural societies women are generally a depressed group. Male dominance is a consequence of their exclusive role in the extra-domestic sphere which fetches them status and freedom to act independently and women are deprived of educational, occupational, social, religious and political rights.

Recently, some anthropologists have taken keen interest in this problem and their studies reveal that in rural societies the women are mainly concerned with the domestic affairs and raising children. Due to which the economic development of those societies is retarded and fertility rate is increased. Subordination of women to men, lack of communication between husband and wife, limited awareness of medical facilities, education and employment facilities, act as obstacles to overall development. On the whole justice to women on social, economic and political fronts is only remedy to uplift the status of women in rural societies. Karl Marx stated that equalization of the sexes is impossible so long as women were excluded from the production work of society and remained restricted to private work.

Over the years the Government of India has been putting efforts to uplift the social status of women and has announced many policies like, reservations in education, jobs and also in political front but still no concrete results has been achieved.

To examine the status of women in terms of criteria like, educational attainment, socio-economic role, health and nutritional conditions, degree of personal autonomy, interpersonal equality, degree of economic control, nature of social and political participation and awareness of equal right, a National Seminar on "Status of Women" in Rural Societies (2nd and 3rd Oct. 2001) was organised by the Department of Anthropology, Dr. H.S.Gour University, Sagar.

To fulfil the above goal, the known specialists in the field were invited to present papers in the seminar. The significant achievement of the seminar was the active participation of the delegates in the panel discussions. After the seminar a pannel of experts were constituted for the formulation of the observations and recommendations of the seminar and authorised Prof. Ramesh Chaube to forward the same to the various social organisations and the government to take steps for the upliftment of the status of women in rural societies. The observations and recommendations made in the Seminar are presented in the last few pages of this book.

We are personally grateful to all the distinguished social scientists who attended the seminar and contributed papers published in this volume and express our deep gratitude to Dr. R.S. Bali, Rtd. Professor of Anthropology, Dr. H.S.Gour University, Sagar for writing foreword of this volume.

We are very much thankful to the Director, Anthropological Survey of India, Calcutta, to provide financial assistance for the organization of the seminar. We are also indebted to the University Grants Commission, New Delhi for providing funds for the publication of this volume.

Ramesh Chaube

Sagar **Kalpana Saini**

Keynote Address

Yogesh Atal

As I stand here I am reminded of the days I spent way back in the late fifties as a student of the first batch of this Department. Of course, at that time this building was not there. Our first classes were held in the barracks of the old campus, and we became the first settlers at the new campus sharing the building of the Applied Geology Department, along with students of the Department of Geography. It is now history that in 1957, the older Department of Anthropogeography was split into two separate entities with Professor S.C. Dube heading the Anthropology Department and Professor S.M. Ali the Department of Geography. As I return to this campus, after lapse of so many years, I cannot help being nostalgic. I am thankful to Professor Chaube for kindly inviting me to this Seminar and thus giving me the opportunity to visit my alma mater.

If there is any reason for my accepting this invitation it is my ties with this institution. I claim no expertise on the subject of the status of rural women. My several years of absence from India when I was working for UNESCO must have made my understanding of the subject obsolete. Thus, while you may find my speech somewhat frustrating, I hope to learn from the deliberations of the Seminar.

Social science interest in the issues related to the status of women is relatively recent. During our student days, as part of the study of the Indian social system—in the tradition of Indology—there used to be some discussion on the status of women in Ancient India. That was based on sacred texts and related only to the Hindus. In the discussion on marriage and family, and on inheritance, the gender aspect was certainly covered; and comparisons were made regarding the practices prevalent in various religious groups as well as in different tribal communities. But the ethnographies did not devote any special chapters on women. It was rare to find any full-length monographs on women. Even Leela Dube's study on the Gond Women was not published.

The status of Women became the prime focus in the 1970's, when the national preparations for the first ever World Conference on Women were initiated. The Government of India also set up a National Committee on the Status of Women. It is the work of this Committee that gave spurt to several studies and reviews of existing literature relative to women. My assignment with the Indian Council of Social Science Research as its first Research Director gave me the opportunity to interact with this Committee and to assist it in its research programme. In fact, the ICSSR commissioned a series of studies on different aspects of the status of women. I was personally involved in the designing of the national study that was undertaken by the Committee.

The Indian effort to portray the status of women was thus a part of the worldwide effort. The designation of the International Year of Women (IYW) and later devotion of an entire decade to women by the international community occasioned a spate of studies and researches. The decade of the 1970's saw the rise of the feminist movement that influenced not only the politics but also the academia. By this time I had joined UNESCO as its Regional Adviser for Social and Human Sciences in Asia and the Pacific. One of my responsibilities was to promote women's studies in social sciences.

During my tenure as Director of the Regional Unit for Social and Human Sciences in Asia-Pacific (RUSHSAP)—nearly nineteen years of its existence—forty-five different studies on various aspects of women in different countries of Asia were carried out resulting in twenty-five monographs, all edited by me. Way back in 1975, I initiated a study involving Bangladesh, India, Republic of Korea, the Philippines, and Thailand which focused on those rural families from where men had migrated to towns. We wanted to find out what happened to women who were left behind temporarily as heads of the households. The resultant book, *Women in Villages, Men in Towns,* was distributed worldwide.

We then carried out a survey of studies on women in the Southeast Asian region. This work was commissioned to Dr. Leela Dube of this very department. She provided a very good bibliography of work done on women in Southeast Asia and identified the gaps that existed in terms of research.

In 1982, I convened a regional meeting in New Delhi to evaluate the present status of women's studies in social sciences and to develop an agenda for future. That meeting was an important landmark because the recommendations that were made by the Group resulted in a series of activities for our Unit. Soon after that meeting, the then Chairperson of the Indian University Grants Commission (UGC), Dr Madhuri Shah, wrote to all the universities in India to carefully read the recommendations of that meeting and offered UGC's support for creating Centres for Women's Studies within the universities. The response to her call was overwhelming; consequently, such centres were set up in a number of universities in India.

One of the recommendations of the meeting was for UNESCO to prepare teaching materials on women's studies and research. If materials do not exist, how could teaching programmes be initiated? These materials were needed for specific country contexts, to be used both by teachers and students for an interdisciplinary course on Women. We succeeded in getting seven country specific teaching materials that included India among others.

We also took steps, following another recommendation of the 1982 meeting, to compile a Directory of Women Social Scientists and another of Institutions engaged in Research on Women.

As I said earlier, several countries prepared reports on the Status of Women for the first World Conference on Women. But some of the countries in the region did not prepare these reports and sought

UNESCO's assistance to prepare them, or update them. Such reports were thus freshly prepared for Afghanistan, People's Republic of China, Lao PDR, Malaysia, Vietnam, Mongolia, and Thailand. These tiny little booklets of about 80 to 120 pages each were also edited by me and published as a UNESCO Series.

I also directed some cross-cultural comparative studies on Women. Following the completion of the study titled, Women in Villages, Men in Towns, a second study on Migration was undertaken again focusing on the families that were left behind when men temporarily migrated to the Middle East for work—the phenomenon was acronymed MIME. Another study on Women: Beyond the Domestic Domain, was undertaken to find out what women were doing outside of their domestic domain and what problems were they experiencing in their new roles in the world of work. This work was done in India, Thailand, and Indonesia. For the study on Women in Politics, research was carried out in five countries: Australia, Bangladesh, India, Malaysia, Nepal, the Philippines, and Thailand. Ewha Women's University and the SNDT Women's University carried out a study based on secondary data on Violence Against Women in the Republic of Korea and in India, respectively.

Preparatory to the International Year of the Family, which was celebrated in 1994, five country studies reviewed the entire literature on family: what has been researched? What areas have been covered? What aspects of the family have been studies? Is family breaking down or getting strong? What is happening to the relationships within the family? The idea was to do stocktaking of researches done on family. That work resulted in a book. The Changing Family in Asia, covering the Philippines, India, Bangladesh, Thailand, and Japan.

Three other studies also related to Women and Family. One was on migrant women in the Metropolitan cities—Beijing, Manila, Bangkok, and New Delhi. A second exercise involved a series of case studies on marginalized women and their reintegration in the economy and the society. And, finally, there was a study of migrant families from the Pacific Island countries settled in New Zealand.

I must say here that in all these studies, with a few exceptions, women social scientists were involved. As I recount these UNESCO efforts to promote studies on women I realize that in many of these exercises India was covered. Thus, UNESCO contributed to the growing literature on Indian women. I feel happy that I was associated with this effort.

While working to promote studies relative to women it became clear that not only was there dearth of scholars specializing in this area, there was also dearth of data on different aspects of women's participation in social, political and economic life. The researchers had to cull out relevant material from various studies that focused on other themes, or to undertake fresh empirical studies. As I mentioned before, ethnographies did discuss the roles of women in different spheres of community life but not specifically focusing on them. They were criticized for the absence of the so-called feminist perspective. Later, when women specific studies were undertaken they mostly concentrated on the urban women; very little work was done on rural women per se.

Women's studies movement that began in the 1970s has now gained a momentum of its own and today one can find several references. An unintended consequence of this has been a rise in the number of women social scientists, and women writers. There are few men who have specialized on women's studies. Such lopsided development is a cause of concern, and is expressed even by some women activists and women social scientists. As a social scientist I strongly feel that neglected areas of study must be prioritized and social scientists be encouraged to undertake researches on those topics. But I do not buy the idea that only "insiders" should undertake such researches.

Let me illustrate this point. When I was in the ICSSR, I was made responsible for implementing a massive all-India study on Education amongst Scheduled Castes and Scheduled Tribes. In all the states of the Indian Union this study was carried out; in each state two projects were commissioned—one for SC and the other for ST students. ICSSR had difficult time finding competent social scientists who were willing to participate in this project by following a common research design and using centrally devised research tools. These project directors were then to be trained. While all this was going on, a starred question was raised in the Parliament seeking the number of SC and ST project directors in the national study. You can well imagine our plight. We in the ICSSR were keen to sponsor research and ensure its successful completion by involving competent social scientists, the politicians were interested in the social demography of the project. The project, to the sure, was to study the problem of education of the SC&ST children, and not to recruit SC&ST project directors. As regards women's studies the same argument holds true. It would be wrong to think that only women can study women for, this would not only mean denial to men who are otherwise competent to specialize in this area, but also keep competent women social scientists solely engaged in women's studies and discourage them from developing other specializations within the social sciences.

In the present context, I would wish to stress the point that there cannot, should not, be a single perspective on women. Their problems should be seen from different disciplinary perspectives, as well as from an interdisciplinary perspective. There is, of course, a place for feminist approach, but that is not all. Social scientists should also resist the temptation of using the social sciences for promoting any ideology. It is all right for the social scientist to work on a topic that is regarded socially, politically, or even ideologically relevant, but it is wrong to be influenced by an ideological or social commitment while researching that topic. The subject must be researched scientifically, maintaining objectivity and value neutrality. Social science is not journalism, nor is it a handmaiden of politics.

The subject of Women's studies has the potential of being ideologically charged. It is therefore essential to emphasize this point about scientific character of social. In several seminars, here in

India and abroad, I have witnessed the discussions on the theme of women that took the form of ideological debates. In such discussions, one finds very little of social science and a good deal of activism. These seminars tend to become forum for the NGOs.

Your Seminar theme relates to the "status" of rural women. The world "status" is a well-development sociological concept. But in the context of women this has been employed in a very journalistic sense. In sociology, a person is supposed to have several statuses and with each status are associated a set of roles vis-a-vis counter statuses. A totality of statuses of a given person is called "status-set" (a concept developed by Robert Merton) or a "station" (as suggested by Kingsley Davis). Writings on the status of women have not used the concept of status in the sociological sense that I just outlined. And yet social scientists working in this area have never bothered to correct their lexicon. The activists have used status to suggest the low and oppressed state of affairs of women compared to men. That is a vulgar and emotionally charged usage. We know that not all women are oppressed, poor, or powerless. We also know that women constitute only a category and not a class in the sociological sense. They derive their socio-economic status (SES) from the family to which they belong, and thus share the SES index value with other members of the family—both male and female. To be sure, there may be differences within the family in terms of other statuses and the associated roles, but these differences cannot be subsumed under one category. In that sense, it will be hazardous to club all the women inhabiting in the rural areas into a single category. We will also have to acknowledge differences in marriage practices, and division of labour between men and women in different castes and tribes. For example, widow remarriage, divorce, and working outside of the home are some of the traits found among lower castes but are denied to women of upper castes. If these traits were to be regarded as desirable, one would find that the women of the so-called Dalit strata are similar to the Western women and thus "modern"; and the process of Sanskritization among them instigates them to discard some of these practices in their effort to emulate the upper castes. Since we constantly make a reference to the western women to unfavourably compare the lot of Indian women, it is pertinent to mention that women's liberation movement originated in the West. To me, this sends the message that the western women also are not liberated. If so, then what is the model to follow?

In saying all this I am not suggesting that all is well. We need to take serious steps to eradicate illiteracy among women, remove all practices of oppression and discrimination, and make them equal partners in the process of development. The key question relates to the model that we ought to follow, or the scenario of the desirable that we must construct. It should be admitted that there does not exist any consensus regarding the desirable, because desirability is value loaded. Social scientists have the responsibility of providing dependable portrayals of the actually existing reality and of working out cost-benefit analysis of alternative strategies proposed by social reformers and activists. But when they indulge in fashioning the scenario of the desirable they enter the realm of values and become committed. While there is nothing wrong in being committed to a set of values, such commitment should be differentiated from commitment to social sciences.

In this regard, let me turn to the currently prevalent debate regarding the reservation of seats for women in the Parliament. I have discussed this in an article published in the *Times of India,* and also in my recent book on the 1999 elections. As social scientists it is our responsibility to point out the pitfalls in any strategy that may be proposed by our politicians. I have argued that personally I am in favour of increasing women's participation in public life, but the modality being recommended by many, of fixing a quota through reservation of seats is questionable not on ideological grounds but on objective criteria. What our politician friends are undermining, knowingly or in ignorance, is the range of unintended consequences that may defeat the very purpose for which the reservation is being proposed. Such questioning is not politically motivated; it is our duty as social scientists to bring this to the notice of our leaders.

I would dare say that now the stage is set for us to move from mere slogan mongering to effective action based on systematic research. We should move from impression to observation and investigation. We should really sincerely rethink many of the issues that have been raised. There is a need to conceptualize this whole dynamic interrelationship between Women and Development. I personally think that in the past, whenever we talked of Women in Development, we talked only of women as passive recipients. But this is not true. They are not only recipients of the fruits of development, but also agents of social change and development. It will be a patronizing attitude to think only of doing something for them; we have to ensure their contribution to society's development.

Thus, the moot question regarding Women and Development is: Is it a one-way relationship or a two-way relationship? Are we talking only of women contributing to social development? Or of women receiving benefits, or otherwise, of Development? Or, is there still another way in which this relationship can be conceptualized? I have no readymade answers, but certainly these are legitimate questions, which must be raised in a forum like this. There are people who equate Development with Modernization, and dissociate the latter from Westernization. In the context of Women, the question is: Does liberation of women mean making women westernized? Or making women modernized? How do we conceptualize development to find out the ideal, the desired destination, for women? What does development really mean? What is the locus particularly of tradition in this development paradigm?

Recent researches have indicated that the dichotomy between tradition and modernity is false. Traditions are not all that bad; nor are all traditions obsolete. Sometimes traditions can also help us modernize. There is an element of modernity in tradition and we need to investigate it. In fact, our study on Women in Villages and Men in Towns, brought home the point that those who went to the urban areas did not only bring some fruits of urbanization to their rural homeland but their departure to the towns resulted in the strengthening of tradition, and cementing of primordial relationships. The visits of the migrant family members were always associated with the celebration of traditional functions and religious festivals. They, therefore, served the function of enhancing family solidarity, of reinforcing kinship ties. In studying women we should not ignore men, nor should we see the relationship between the two genders as exploitative. It will be interesting to see conflictual relationship between women. The current serial on Star TV, *Kyunki Saas bhi Kabhi Bahu thi* is not fictional. Similarly it will be interesting to see how women of higher class treat women of the lower class. When we study women in their roles outside the domestic domain, we find that they generally complain of discrimination against them by men, but the same women mistreat their maidservants at home. The relationship between the housewife and the maid is a good example of contradiction between the word and the deed. Women exploit women; and this point is never highlighted by those who plead for women's lib. I would urge that these kinds of questions, though disturbing, should also be investigated.

I have spoken to you as a fellow researcher. That is why I tried to raise some critical issues that need reflection and research. I am confident that this Seminar will reach a very successful conclusion, and that some useful follow-up actions will be taken up.

List of Contributors

Ramesh Chaube	:	Professor and Head Department of Anthropology Dr. H.S. Gour University, Sagar.
Dr. (Mrs.) Kalpana Saini	:	Reader, Department of Anthropology H.S. Gour University, Sagar (M.P.).
Dr. M.K. Choudhuri	:	Director, Cultural Research Institute, Backward Classes Welfare Department Government of West Bengal.
Premanand Panda	:	Sambalpur University, Sambalpur.
Dr. N.K. Das	:	Anthropological Survey of India, Field Station, Sagar (M.P.)-470 003.
Surendra Kumar Gupta	:	Retired Professor, Department Sociology of and Social Antropology Punjabi University Patiala.
Dr. B.R. Rizvi	:	Deputy Director Anthropological Survey of India, Western Regional Centre, Udaipur-313001.
G.D. Pandey	:	Regional Medical Research Centre (for Tribals) Indian Counsil of Medical Research Nagpur Road Jabalpur.
A.N. Sandhwar	:	University Professor, Department of Anthropology, Ranchi University Ranchi.
Prof. V.D. Jha	:	Prof. and Head Department of Ancient Indian History Culture and Archaeology, Dean, Faculty of Social Science, Dr. H.S. Gour University Sagar.
Harapriya Samanataraya	:	Principle, Womens College Padampur, Dist. Bargarh.

D. Sun	:	Anthropological Survey of India Sagar Field Station Sagar.
Dipak K. Adok	:	Anthropological Survey of India Field Station Sagar.
Alok Chantia	:	Lecturer (Anthropology), Jai Narayan P.G. College, Lucknow.
Prof. A.R.N. Shrivastava	:	Professor and Head Department of Anthropology, University of Allahabad.
Dr. Sangeeta Sinha	:	Lecturer in Sociology at Government P.G. College Chakia (Chandauli District).
ए. एच. सी. जैन	:	प्रो. सतत् शिक्षा एवं विस्तार विभाग डा. हरीसिंह गौर विश्वविद्यालय सागर
डा. वद्रीप्रसाद	:	भाषा विज्ञान विभाग, डा. हरीसिंह गौर विश्वविद्यालय, सागर
डा. श्रीनाथ शर्मा	:	अध्यक्ष, समाजशास्त्र विभाग, डा. हरीसिंह गौर विश्वविद्यालय, सागर
डा. अनिल जैन	:	सहायक प्राध्यापक (वाणिज्य), शासकीय स्नातकोत्तर महाविद्यालय, बीना, (सागर) (म.प्र.)
डा. एस. के. त्रिपाठी	:	सहायक प्राध्यापक (अंग्रेजी), शासकीय स्नातकोत्तर महाविद्यालय, बीना, (सागर) (म.प्र.)

1

Status of Rural Women with Special Reference to Women of Scheduled Communities - A Situational Analysis

M.K. Choudhuri • Kalpana Saini

After celebrating the Golden Jubilee year of Independence a few years' back, India enter into the new millennium traversing a meandering path through ups and downs and light and shadows.

Many changes have taken place in all spheres of life. Scientific and technological development, impact of industrialisation, urbanisation, influence of Western Education, impact of British rule and finally the new economic policy of Globalisation have marked a perceptible change in the socio-economic and political scenario of Indian Society. Consequently ideas and values, manners and customs, life and culture have undergone a drastic modification resulting a thrust on the age old tradition of Indian Civilization. But this thrust of change is not uniform among all the sections of population as the major share of the technological development was shared by the urban mass depriving the rural population. In spite of this technological and scientific development, the age old social values of gender discrimination is still persisting in our country. Various women liberation movements were launched to pacify this gender bias issue but domination of male is still in vogue specially in the patriarchate Indian society. This age old value of male supremacy is nurtured resulting in deprivation of the women folk in every sphere of life. The women are not getting proper status for performing their specific role in the society.

In the field of economy and education, the female population specially the rural females are lagging much behind and condition of the Scheduled Caste and Scheduled Tribe Women is still grave.

As per Census 1991, most of the women live in rural areas, who are yet to come out from the age old traditions. They mainly engaged in agriculture and allied sector as labourers and in household industry as workers. Among these women folk, there are differences between Scheduled Castes, Scheduled Tribes and Other Communities, i.e., non-Scheduled Communities.

Thus, before going to the subject, it is necessary to review the socio-economic condition of the rural women in general and women belong to scheduled communities in particular, as this will help us to understand the matrix of the present status of the women folk of our country.

In India, of the total female population, 74.25 per cent live in rural areas, and among 31 states and Union Territories, highest percentage of rural women out of the total women of the respective State/UT is observed in Dadra and Nagar Haveli with 92.19 and lowest in Chandigarh (9.65). On the basis of relative concentration (Rural female percentage to total female of each State/UTs). 20 States/UTs have more than 70 per cent rural female population.

Similarly among the Scheduled Castes population of India, 81.46 per cent live in rural areas, whereas among the Scheduled Tribes the said percentage is 92.81. All these indicate that females in general and females of Scheduled population in particular, mostly inhabitate in rural India. Table 1.1 describes in details.

TABLE : 1.1

ALL INDIA DISTRIBUTION OF RURAL FEMALE POPULATION BY STATES & UNION TERRITORIES

Sr.	State	All Pop.	All Pop. (per cent)	SC Pop.	SC Pop. (per cent)	ST Pop.	ST Pop. (per cent)
01	Andhra Pradesh	32783427	73.30	5212412	82.63	2056664	92.58
02	Arunachal Pradesh	399554	88.34	1561	68.93	274954	94.43
03	Assam	10756333	89.46	794795	86.35	1412881	96.82
04	Bihar	41172374	87.38	6002340	91.28	3259351	93.20
05	Goa	575003	59.80	11975	52.34	177	23.16
06	Gujarat	19954373	66.05	1470672	62.42	3029828	92.09
07	Haryana	7636174	75.32	1503112	82.30	0	0.00
08	Himachal Pradesh	2553410	92.01	644241	94.05	108109	97.84
09	Karnataka	22025284	69.58	3613210	76.83	938947	85.24
10	Kerala	14809523	73.64	1463908	81.46	160155	96.65
11	Madhya Pradesh	31913877	77.33	4598873	78.33	7640860	95.37
12	Maharashtra	38111569	62.60	4252467	63.85	3600498	87.88
13	Manipur	898790	72.22	18299	47.16	309453	91.53
14	Meghalaya	867091	81.87	4091	55.61	757693	86.08
15	Mizoram	330778	53.63	94	60.64	323746	54.33

(Contd.)

16	Nagaland	568264	84.31	0	0.00	515666	88.15
17	Orissa	15595590	87.40	2532850	89.52	3519323	95.05
18	Punjab	9503935	70.70	2676857	79.45	0	0.00
19	Rajasthan	20963210	77.53	3600600	80.33	2637867	95.69
20	Sikkim	190030	91.66	11660	88.51	43397	92.19
21	Tamil Nadu	27559971	66.09	5297667	78.69	281182	87.97
22	Tripura	1339275	84.59	219600	84.06	419120	98.43
23	Uttar Pradesh	65075330	80.38	13677277	88.37	137481	94.47
24	West Bengal	32567332	73.47	7753779	84.95	1869805	95.03
	Union Territories						
01	Andaman & Nicobar Islands	126292	74.21	0	0.00	13020	98.56
02	Chandigarh	283401	9.05	47423	12.76	0	0.00
03	Dadra & Nagar Haveli	67524	92.19	1312	82.55	55278	96.89
04	Daman & Diu	49991	51.87	2009	62.27	5651	78.02
05	Delhi	4265132	9.94	816146	11.49	0	0.00
06	Lakshadweep	25089	44.10	0	0.00	24003	44.79
07	Pondicherry	399704	35.83	65087	59.19	0	0.00
	All India (Excluding J & K)	**403367630**	**74.75**	**66294317**	**81.46**	**33395109**	**92.81**

As stated earlier, among the rural women population of each State and Union Territories, certain percentage of women belong to scheduled communities. According to the Census (1991) there are 3 (three) States and Union Territories where no Scheduled Castes population has been recorded. In all, Scheduled Castes population is observed only in 28 States and UTs. Similarly, not a single person was recorded as Scheduled Tribe in 5 States and UTs, thus, altogether the concerned population was noted only in 26 States/UTs. Among the total rural female population of each States/UTs the percentage of Scheduled Castes female is highest in Punjab with 31.65 per cent followed by West Bengal (27.53) and Pondichery (26.90). In case of Scheduled Tribes rural females the highest is recorded in Mizoram with 99.16 per cent, closely followed by Lakshadweep (97.17), Nagaland (94.88) and Meghalaya (91.88). In fact, the North-Eastern States are generally dominated by Scheduled Tribes population and majority of them live in rural areas. According to 1991 census of the total rural female population, Scheduled Castes and Scheduled Tribes constitute 17.91 and 10.28 per cent respectively. To get a clear picture of rural female population of different States/UTs Table 1.2 May be seen.

TABLE : 1.2

PROPORTIONATE DISTRIBUTION OF SC AND ST FEMALES IN RURAL INDIA

Sr.	*State*	*All Females*	*SC Pop (F) (per cent)*	*St Pop (F) (per cent)*
1	2	3	4	5
01	Andhra Pradesh	24029007	17.92	7.92
02	Arunachal Pradesh	352964	0.30	73.56
03	Assam	9622366	7.13	14.22
04	Bihar	35976358	15.23	8.44
05	Goa	343872	1.82	0.01
06	Gujarat	13179222	6.97	21.17

(Contd.)

1	2	3	4	5
07	Haryana	5751570	21.51	0.00
08	Himachal Pradesh	2349488	25.79	4.50
09	Karnataka	15324471	18.11	5.22
10	Kerala	10905436	10.93	1.42
11	Madhya Pradesh	24677980	14.60	29.53
12	Maharashtra	23859321	11.38	13.26
13	Manipur	649109	1.33	43.64
14	Meghalaya	709866	0.32	91.88
15	Mizoram	177396	0.03	99.16
16	Nagaland	479088	0.00	94.88
17	Orissa	13629798	16.63	24.54
18	Punjab	6719321	31.65	0.00
19	Rajasthan	16252414	17.80	15.53
20	Sikkim	174174	5.93	22.97
21	Tamil Nadu	18213637	22.89	1.36
22	Tripura	1132955	16.29	36.41
23	Uttar Pradesh	52309234	23.11	0.25
24	West Bengal	23928154	27.53	7.43
	Union Territories			
01	Andaman & Nicobar Islands	93720	0.00	13.69
02	Chandigarh	25638	23.60	0.00
03	Dadra & Nagar Haveli	62253	1.74	86.04
04	Daman & Diu	25932	4.82	17.00
05	Delhi	423963	22.11	0.00
06	Lakshadweep	11063	0.00	97.17
07	Pondicherry	143201	26.90	0.00
	All India (Excluding J & K)	**301532971**	**17.91**	**10.28**

* Excludes Figures of Jammu & Kashmir where 1991 Census was not taken.

Sex ratio of average population is an important parameter in understanding the Demographic pattern of the concerned population. It is interesting to note that female birth is still not welcome by the Indian communities. Parents without a son is not desirable even in this present generation, so either at the time of birth or by sex-determination test male-dominated society prefers to make an end of that girl to be born. This is a common practice throughout the country, save and except in the case of Scheduled Tribe, where a girl child has a significant position in the society. Among the tribal folk there is less discrimination between a boy and a girl. According to their socio—cultural customs, a boy has to pay bride price during marriage as he is taking away an economic hand from a family which will be his additional value. General sex ratio of women folk is 927, which is 922 in case of Scheduled Castes and 972 among the Scheduled Tribes. It has been observed that there are 9 States and UTs where the female birth is less than 900, on the other hand in Kerala, it is more than 1000. Among the Scheduled Castes, low sex ratio is recorded in 7 States and UTs and lowest is in Arunachal Pradesh with 627 and highest in Kerala with 1029. In case of Scheduled Tribes there is only one State, i.e., Goa where sex—ratio is less than 900. Maximum Scheduled Tribe female population per 1000 males has been observed in Dadra & Nagar Haveli. The sex-ratio of three sections of female population clearly supported the observation made in the previous para. Table 1.3 gives a detailed idea on the sex radio of different states/UTs.

TABLE : 1.3

DISTRIBUTION OF SEX RATIO BY STATES/UTS

Sl. No.	*India/State or Union Territory*	*Sex Ratio (Females per 1000 Males)*		
		Total Population	*Scheduled Castes Population*	*Scheduled Tribes Population*
(1)	(2)	(3)	(4)	(5)
	INDIA*	927	922	972
	STATES			
01	Andhra Pradesh	972	969	960

(Contd.)

(1)	(2)	(3)	(4)	(5)
02	Arunachal Pradesh	859	627	998
03	Assam	923	919	967
04	Bihar	911	914	971
05	Goa	967	967	889
06	Gujarat	934	925	967
07	Haryana	865	860	-
08	Himachal Pradesh	976	967	981
09	Karnataka	960	962	961
10	Kerala	1,036	1,029	996
11	Madhya Pradesh	931	915	985
12	Maharashtra	934	944	968
13	Manipur	958	973	959
14	Meghalaya	955	821	997
15	Mizoram	921	157	982
16	Nagaland	886	-	946
17	Orissa	971	975	1,002
18	Punjab	882	873	-
19	Rajasthan	910	899	930
20	Sikkim	878	939	914
21	Tamil Nadu	974	978	960
22	Tripura	945	949	965
23	Uttar Pradesh	879	877	914
24	West Bengal	917	931	964
	Union Territories			
01	Andaman & Nicobar Islands	818	-	947
02	Chandigarh	790	810	-
03	Dadra & Nagar Haveli	952	925	1,022
04	Daman & Diu	969	1,067	931
05	Delhi	827	834	-
06	Lakshadweep	943	-	994
07	Pondicherry	979	983	-

* Excludes Figures of Jammu & Kashmir where 1991 Census was not taken.

By examining the Census reports, one may observe the percentage of rural women in general and can identify the States with Very High or Low rural female population but it may not be so easy to review the percentage of Scheduled Castes or Scheduled Tribes women population, whether Very High or Low in the context of rural women folk of that State or UTs. Thus, keeping the population of rural women in one hand, one may get the population percentages of Scheduled Castes, Scheduled Tribes women. To understand this population distribution, both the rural Scheduled Castes and Scheduled Tribes women are classified into four (4) categories. Very High, High. Low and Very Low according to the Quartile value (Q_1, Q_2, Q_3) based on their population percentage.

Table 1.4 deals with general rural female with Scheduled Castes rural female and it reveals that there are 8 States/UTs where percentage of rural women is more than 84.06 per cent but of them only in Himchal Pradesh, the rural Scheduled Castes female population is very high (above 22.20). On the other hand percentage of rural women is very High in Arunachal Pradesh and Dadra and Nagar Haveli but the percentage of Scheduled Castes rural women is Very Low (less than 5.62).

TABLE : 1.4

DISTRIBUTION OF RURAL WOMEN AND SCEHEDULED CASTE WOMEN BY STATES/UTS

	SCHEDULED CASTES			
Rural Women (General)	Very High (22.2)	High (15.6-22.1)	Low (5.63-15.5)	Very Low (-5.62)
(1)	(2)	(3)	(4)	(5)
Very High (84.06+)	Himachal Pradesh	Tripura Orissa	Assam Sikkim Bihar	Arunachal Pradesh Dadra Nagar Haveli
High	Uttar	Haryana	Madhya	Meghalaya

(Contd.)

(Contd.)

(1)	(2)	(3)	(4)	(5)
(75.00-84.05)	Pradesh	Rajasthan	Pradesh	
Low	Tamil Nadu	Karnataka	Kerala	Manipur
(61.88-74.99)	Punjab		Gujarat	
	West Bengal		Andhra Pradesh	
			Maharashtra	
Very Low (-61.87)	Chandigarh Pondichery	Delhi	-	Goa Daman Diu Mizoram
	7	6	8	7

*No S.C. Population :- Nagaland, Andaman Nicobar Island, Lakshadweep.

Range :- 0.03 (Mizoram), 27.53 (West Bengal)

Similarly, there are 7 States/UTs where percentage of Scheduled Castes rural women is above 22.20, but amongst them there are only three States, i.e., Tamil Nadu, Punjab and West Bengal where the percentage of rural Scheduled Castes women is Very High.

Table 1.5 reveals the similar picture between the rural women in general and Scheduled Tribes rural women. Out of 26 States/UTs where Scheduled Tribes population were recorded, Very High Scheduled Tribes rural women are noted in 7 States/UTs and out of those, three States/UTs fall under Very High rural female category. These are Nagaland, Arunachal Pradesh and Dadra Nagar Haveli.

These two tables will help the researcher, planner and administrators either to conduct studies in those States/UTs or taking development programmes for the concerned population.

TABLE : 1.5

DISTRIBUTION OF RURAL WOMEN AND SCEHEDULED TRIBES WOMEN BY STATES/UTS

SCHEDULED CASTES				
Rural Women (General)	Very High (42.50+)	High (17.50-42.49)	Low (6.88-17.49)	Very Low (-6.88)
(1)	(2)	(3)	(4)	(5)
Very High (84.06+)	Nagaland Arunachal Pradesh Dadra Nagar Haveli	Tripura Orissa Sikkim	Assam Bihar	Himachal Pradesh
High (75.00-84.05)	Meghalaya	Madhya Pradesh	Rajasthan	Uttar Pradesh
Low (61.88-74.99)	Manipur	Gujarat	Andaman Nicobar Island Andhra Pradesh West Bengal Maharashtra	Kerala Tamil Nadu Karnataka
Very Low (-61.87)	Lakhadweep Mizoram	Daman Diu	Goa	
	7	5	8	6

Note : - No. S.T. Population : - Haryana, Punjab, Chandigarh, Delhi Pondichery.

S.T. Lowest : Goa (0.01), Highest : Mizoram (99.16)

Education is one of the important social factors to identify the social status of a community or a section of population. It is more essential if one likes to bring any positive change in the socio-economic and cultural aspects of the concerned population belong to any Caste, Class or Community. According to the traditional values, parents generally sent their sons to schools but not their girls. Further, in rural life, girls are supposed to assist not only in household jobs

TABLE : 2.1

LITERACY RATE OF MALES AND FEMALES BY STATES/UTS

Sl. No	*India/State or Union Territory*	*Males*			*Females*		
		Total	*SC*	*ST*	*Total*	*SC*	*ST*
(1)	*(2)*	*(3)*	*(4)*	*(5)*	*(6)*	*(7)*	*(8)*
	INDIA*	64.13	49.19	40.65	39.29	23.76	18.19
	STATES						
01	Andhra Pradesh	55.13	41.88	25.25	32.72	20.92	8.68
02	Arunachal Pradesh	51.45	66.25	44.00	29.69	41.42	24.94
03	Assam	61.87	63.88	58.93	43.03	42.99	38.98
04	Bihar	52.49	30.64	38.40	22.89	7.07	14.75
05	Goa	83.64	69.55	54.43	67.09	47.51	29.01
06	Gujarat	73.13	75.47	48.25	48.64	45.54	24.20
07	Haryana	69.10	52.06	-	40.47	24.15	
08	Himachal Pradesh	75.36	64.98	62.74	52.13	41.02	31.18
09	Karnataka	67.26	49.69	47.95	44.34	25.95	23.57
10	Kerala	93.62	85.22	63.38	86.13	74.31	51.07
11	Madhya Pradesh	58.42	50.51	32.16	28.85	18.11	10.73
12	Maharashtra	76.56	70.45	49.09	52.32	41.59	24.03
13	Manipur	71.63	65.28	62.39	47.60	47.41	44.48

(1)	(2)	(3)	(4)	(5)	(6)	(7)	(8)
14	Meghalaya	53.12	54.56	49.78	44.85	31.19	43.63
15	Mizoram	85.61	77.54	86.67	78.60	81.25	78.74
16	Nagaland	67.62	-	66.27	54.27	-	54.51
17	Orissa	63.09	52.42	34.44	34.68	20.74	10.21
18	Punjab	65.66	49.82	-	50.41	31.03	-
19	Rajasthan	54.99	42.38	33.29	20.44	8.31	4.42
20	Sikkim	65.74	58.69	66.80	46.69	42.77	50.37
21	Tamil Nadu	73.75	58.36	35.25	51.33	34.89	20.23
22	Tripura	70.58	67.25	52.88	49.65	45.45	27.34
23	Uttar Pradesh	55.73	40.80	49.95	25.31	10.69	19.86
24	West Bengal	67.81	54.55	40.07	46.56	28.87	14.98
	Union Territories						
01	Andaman & Nicobar Islands	78.99	-	64.16	65.46	-	48.74
02	Chandigarh	82.04	64.74	-	72.34	43.54	-
03	Dadra & Nagar Haveli	53.56	88.03	40.75	26.98	66.61	15.94
04	Daman & Diu	82.66	91.85	63.58	59.40	67.62	41.45
05	Delhi	82.01	68.77	-	66.99	43.82	-
06	Lakshadweep	90.18	-	89.50	72.89	-	71.71
07	Pondicherry	83.68	66.10	-	65.63	46.28	-

*Excludes Figures of Jammu & Kashmir where 1991 Census was not taken.

but also in keeping their youngers when the parents go out for work. Due to this age old tradition, since historical past females are lagging behind from the males, which is more significant in case of rural areas than the urban areas.

Table 2.1 describes the literacy rate at both males and females of General, Scheduled Caste and Scheduled Tribes population of different States/UTs of the country. The general literacy rate of Indian population is 52.21 whereas among the Scheduled Castes and Scheduled Tribes the said percentages are as low as 37.41 and 29.60 respectively. It may only be stated that in respect of States & UTs, Scheduled Castes literacy rate is quite below from the average literacy rate (52.21) noted for India and in case of Scheduled Tribes, only 8 States and UTs are above that average rate noted for India. If one examine the sexwise literacy status may find a wide difference between the males and the females and also among the three sections of population. All these facts reveal that females in general are yet to be at par with the males and the said scenario is more gloomy among the female population of scheduled communities and tribe in particular. In view of this, if one examines the literacy rate of the rural female and also of the concerned population belong to scheduled communities may observe a different picture.

Out of 31 States and UTs, lowest literacy percentage among the rural women has been recorded in Chandigarh (5.51) and highest percentage is observed in Himachal Pradesh with 87.72. The average literacy rate of rural women among the rural female population of India is 57.75 per cent as per 1991 census. It may be observed from the Table 2.2 that though the literacy status of the tribal rural women population is apparently better in compression to other two sections or rural female population. Among the Scheduled Castes females, the lowest rate is 9.78 per cent has been recorded in Delhi and highest in Himachal Pradesh with 91.12 per cent. Of the Scheduled Tribes females, the said percentages are noted in Goa with 5.02 per cent and in Andaman Nicobar Islands with 97.38 per cent. Here it may be mentioned that as the population of the country inhabitate mainly in rural areas thus this literacy status does not indicate the true picture for getting the actual status of female literacy.

TABLE : 2.2

PROPORATION LITERACY RATES OF ALL INDIAN RURAL FEMALES

Sr.	*State*	*RUR. LIT. (F)* (per cent	*SC LIT. (RF)* (per cent)	*ST LIT. (RF)* (per cent)
01	Andhra Pradesh	53.32	63.76	77.65
1	2	3	3	4
02	Arunachal Pradesh	75.15	61.43	86.75
03	Assam	80.85	81.24	93.99
04	Bihar	68.19	71.42	80.59
05	Goa	56.10	48.92	5.26
06	Gujarat	52.15	53.53	87.31
07	Haryana	60.06	76.57	0.00
08	Himachal Pradesh	87.72	91.12	94.85
09	Karnataka	54.16	56.55	72.42
10	Kerala	72.53	79.97	95.73
11	Madhya Pradesh	52.48	57.39	86.49
12	Maharashtra	48.57	52.08	72.69
13	Manipur	65.27	46.39	86.62
14	Meghalaya	66.83	43.33	73.75
15	Mizoram	45.12	65.38	45.70
16	Nagaland	77.94	0.00	82.63
17	Orissa	77.46	83.75	86.53
18	Punjab	61.40	74.76	0.00
19	Rajasthan	43.70	45.74	78.70
20	Sikkim	85.96	80.23	87.58

(Contd.)

(Contd.)

21	Tamil Nadu	53.63	68.20	77.40
22	Tripura	74.73	80.40	94.85
23	Uttar Pradesh	60.11	69.99	85.18
24	West Bengal	58.95	76.98	89.18
U1	Andaman & Nicobar Islands	69.63	0.00	97.38
U2	Chandigarh	5.51	10.13	0.00
U3	Dadra & Nagar Haveli	79.30	83.60	92.35
U4	Daman & Diu	39.69	66.20	76.34
U5	Delhi	7.35	9.78	0.00
U6	Lakshadweep	41.15	0.00	42.12
U7	Pondicherry	28.97	50.64	0.00
	All India (Excluding J & K)	**57.75**	**66.52**	**81.58**

To review or to have clear understanding Table 2.3 is to be consulted, which describes the literacy rate of the rural women of the total female literacies. Accordingly, keeping the women concentration in one hand and the literacy rate on the other, if it is examined as per quartile values, one may finds from the Table 2.4 that there are 8 States and UTs with Very High rural women concentration and Very High literacy rate. In this connection, it may also be noted that except Orissa and Dadra & Nagar Haveli all other States belong to North Eastern Region. Another exception is Kerala State, where rural women percentage may be low but the literacy rate is Very High. It clearly indicates that it is necessary to improve the literacy percentage among the rural women in different States/ UTs.

Similarly, among the Scheduled Caste rural women there are eight (8) States and UTs having Very High literacy rate but amongst these six (6) have Very High concentration and Very High literacy rate too.

TABLE : 2.3

DISTRIBUTION OF ALL INDIA RURAL FEMALE LITERATE POPULATION BY SC AND ST

Sl. No	*State*	*All Literates (per cent*	*SC LIT. (F) (per cent)*	*ST LIT. (F) (per cent)*
01	Andhra Pradesh	23.92	11.92	2.30
02	Arunachal Pradesh	25.31	0.44	67.48
03	Assam	39.19	7.43	13.77
04	Bihar	17.95	4.60	6.09
05	Goa	62.87	1.23	0.00
06	Gujarat	38.65	7.02	12.30
07	Haryana	32.51	14.46	0.00
08	Himachal Pradesh	49.79	20.20	2.69
09	Karnataka	34.76	9.70	2.95
10	Kerala	85.12	9.42	0.83
11	Madhya Pradesh	19.73	9.74	14.37
12	Maharashtra	40.96	9.33	6.26
13	Manipur	43.26	1.44	42.80
14	Meghalaya	37.12	0.21	93.33
15	Mizoram	67.03	0.04	99.36
16	Nagaland	50.36	0.00	96.10
17	Orissa	30.79	10.37	7.25
18	Punjab	43.85	20.39	0.00
19	Rajasthan	11.59	7.15	4.81
20	Sikkim	43.98	5.21	25.32
21	Tamil Nadu	41.84	16.18	0.56
22	Tripura	44.33	15.83	21.32

(Contd.)

(Contd.)

23	Uttar Pradesh	19.02	10.16	0.23
24	West Bengal	38.12%	18.89%	2.72
	UNION TERRITORIES			
01	Andaman & Nicobar Islands	61.99	0.00	10.95
02	Chandigarh	47.83	17.37	0.00
03	Dadra & Nagar Haveli	23.30	5.46	55.84
04	Daman & Diu	46.70	7.55	14.83
05	Delhi	52.15	15.90	0.00
06	Lakshadweep	68.72	0.00	96.03
07	Pondicherry	53.96	19.49	0.00
	All India (Excluding J & K)	**30.62**	**11.20**	**5.27**

TABLE : 2.4

DISTRIBUTION OF RURAL WOMEN LITERATES BY RURAL WOMEN POPULATION

	Rural Women Literacy			
Rural Female Population	Very High (72.09+)	High (72.08-60.72)	Low (60.71-49.38)	Very Low (49.37-5.51)
(1)	(2)	(3)	(4)	(5)
Very High (84.06+)	Nagaland Tripural Orissa Arunachal Pradesh Assam Sikkim Himachal Pradesh Dadra Nagar Haveli	Bihar	-	-

(1)	(2)	(3)	(4)	(5)
High (75.00-84.05)	-	Meghalaya	Madhya Pradesh Uttar Pradesh Haryana	Rajasthan
Low (61.88-74.99)	Kerala	Manipur Andaman Nicobar Island	Gujarat Tamil Nadu Karnataka Punjab Andhra Pradesh West Bengal	Maharashtra
Very Low (-61.87)	-	-	Goa	Daman Diu Chandigarh Delhi Pondichery Lakshadweep Mizoram
	9	4	10	8

These States are Himachal Pradesh, Punjab, Tamil Nadu, West Bangal, Chandigarh and Pondichery. Though in all 10 States and UTs are above the average rate noted for India (11.20 per cent). For further clarification Table 2.5 may be consulted.

TABLE : 2.5

DISTRIBUTION OF SC LITERATES BY SC RURAL WOMEN

	Scheduled Caste Literacy Percentage (Female)			
SC Female Population	Very High (15.0+)	High (8.50-14.99)	Low (5.01-8.40)	Very Low (5.50+)
(1)	(2)	(3)	(4)	(5)
Very High (22.20+)	Himachal Pradesh Punjab Tamil Nadu West Bengal	Uttar Pradesh		- -

(1)	(2)	(3)	(4)	(5)
	Chandigarh Pondichery			
High (75.00-84.05)	Tripura Delhi	Haryana Karnataka Orissa	Rajasthan	
Low (61.88-74.99)	-	Andhra Pradesh Kerala Madhya Pradesh Maharashtra	Assam Gujarat Sikkaim	Bihar
Very Low (-61.87)	-	-	Dadra Nagar Haveli Daman and Diu	Arunachal Pradesh Goa Manipur Meghalaya Mizoram
	8	8	6	6

In case of Scheduled Tribes women of rural India, the said literacy percentage of the rural Scheduled Tribes women is Very High in most of the N.E. States apart from Dadra & Nagar Haveli and Lakshadweep. For better understanding Table 2.6 may be seen, which reveals that there are 5 States and 2 UTs having Very High rural women population and also Very High literacy rate. These are Arunachal Pradesh, Manipur, Meghalaya, Mizoram, Nagaland, Dadra & Nagar Haveli and Lakshadweep.

TABLE : 2.6

DISTRIBUTION OF SCHEDULED TRIBE LITERATES BY SCHEDULED TRIBE RURAL WOMEN

	Scheduled Tribe Literacy Percentage (Female)			
ST Rural Women Population	Very High (42.50+)	High (11.00-42.49)	Low (4.08-10.99)	Very Low (4.47)
(1)	(2)	(3)	(4)	(5)
Very High (42.50+)	Arunachal Pradesh			Punjab Chandigarh

(1)	(2)	(3)	(4)	(5)
	Manipur Meghalaya Mizoram Nagaland Dadra Nagar Haveli Lakshadweep			Pondichery Delhi Haryana
High (17.50-42.49)	-	Gujarat Madhya Pradesh Sikkim Tripura	Orissa	
Low (6.88-17.49)	-	Assam Daman Diu	Bihar Maharashtra Rajasthan Andaman Nicobar Island	Andhra Pradesh West Bengal
Very Low (-6.87)	Tamil Nadu Uttar Pradesh	-	-	Goa Himachal Pradesh Karnataka Kerala
	9	6	5	6

From all these three tables, it may be stated that Scheduled Castes literacy percentage of all the States/UTs fall in the Very Low category in relation to General rural women literacy rate. On the other hand, there are 4 States/UTs (Nagaland, Mizoram, Manipur and Lakshadweep) where the literacy rate of the rural Scheduled Tribes women is Very High even in comparison to general women literacy rate. In the same scale, Arunachal Pradesh also fall in High literacy category. Here, mention may be made that all these N.E. States are tribal dominated States.

Considering all these facts and figures, it is quite clear that educational status of rural women is still to go a long way, specially to be at par with their male counterpart. This is more in case of women belong to Scheduled Castes and Scheduled Tribes. In view of the Rural and Urban literacy rate, one may observe that percentage of literates among rural women is higher thanthat of urban areas,

TABLE : 3.1

SEX WISE DISTRIBUTION OF WORKERS BY THREE SECTIONS OF POPULATION

WORK PARTICIPATION RATE (Total Workers as percentage of total population)

Sl. No.	India State of Union Territory	Persons			Males			Females		
		Total Population	Scheduled Castes Population	Scheduled Tribes Population	Total Population	Scheduled Castes Population	Scheduled Tribes Population	Total Population	Scheduled Castes Population	Scheduled Tribes Population
1	2	3	4	5	6	7	8	9	10	11
	India	37.46	39.25	49.30	51.55	51.48	54.74	22.25	25.98	43.71
	STATES									
01	Andhra Pradesh	45.05	51.08	54.01	55.48	55.31	57.30	34.32	46.71	50.63
02	Arunachal Pradesh	46.24	44.27	45.85	53.76	64.27	47.61	37.49	12.36	44.09
03	Assam	36.09	34.40	41.19	49.45	49.36	48.29	21.61	18.13	33.84
04	Bihar	32.16	37.40	45.67	47.92	50.11	53.39	14.86	23.50	37.72
05	Goa	35.28	38.07	37.77	49.56	49.62	55.28	20.52	26.12	18.08
06	Gujarat	40.23	37.61	51.70	53.57	48.39	56.33	25.96	25.95	46.91
07	Haryana	31.00	30.97	-	48.51	47.59	-	10.76	11.63	-
08	Himachal Pradesh	42.83	43.44	49.55	50.64	51.00	53.39	34.81	35.63	45.64
09	Karnataka	41.99	44.66	47.80	54.09	52.40	55.72	29.39	36.62	39.56
10	Kerala	31.43	41.21	46.04	47.56	50.96	56.14	15.85	31.73	36.90
11	Madhya Pradesh	42.82	43.42	52.67	52.26	50.88	56.95	32.68	35.27	48.32
12	Maharashtra	42.97	42.82	52.23	52.17	49.11	54.73	33.11	36.16	49.66

(Contd.)

(Contd..)

13 Manipur	42.18	48.96	46.67	45.27	46.71	47.33	38.96	30.99	45.97
14 Meghalaya	42.67	35.71	43.21	50.07	53.64	48.63	34.93	13.88	37.78
15 Mizoram	48.91	79.16	47.56	53.87	89.95	51.08	43.52	10.64	43.98
16 Nagaland	42.68	-	41.96	46.86	-	41.68	37.96	-	40.15
17 Orissa	37.53	39.26	49.36	53.79	54.69	58.94	20.79	23.44	39.81
18 Punjab	30.88	30.71	-	54.22	52.81	-	4.40	5.40	-
19 Rajasthan	38.87	39.26	46.42	49.30	48.58	51.81	27.40	28.89	40.63
20 Sikkim	41.51	38.55	40.45	51.26	49.57	48.58	30.41	26.80	31.56
21 Tamil Nadu	43.31	48.43	52.10	56.39	55.78	59.39	29.89	40.93	44.51
22 Tripura	31.14	28.69	35.80	47.55	47.43	45.93	13.76	8.91	25.32
23 Uttar Pradesh	32.20	35.29	43.42	49.68	50.80	53.04	12.32	17.61	32.90
24 West Bengal	32.19	33.31	47.66	54.40	52.03	54.05	11.25	13.32	41.03
UNION TERRITORIES									
01 Andaman & Nicobar Islands	35.24	-	39.15	53.32	-	50.25	13.13	-	27.43
02 Chandigarh	34.94	32.38	-	54.34	50.80	-	10.39	9.51	-
03 Dadra & Nagar Haveli	53.25	38.94	55.63	57.50	50.07	55.80	48.79	26.91	55.46
04 Daman & Diu	37.63	29.43	4742	51.63	41.71	53.86	23.17	17.92	40.49
05 Delhi	31.64	29.25	-	51.72	47.40	-	7.36	7.49	-
06 Lakshadweep	26.41	-	24.06	44.17	-	40.67	7.60	-	9.33
07 Pondicherry	33.08	40.80	-	50.55	50.99	-	15.24	30.53	-

*Excludes Figures of Jammu & Kashmir where 1991 census was not taken.

because of the fact that the women belong to scheduled population mainly come to urban areas as workers for earning only. Neither they nor their children get the opportunity to avail this facility. Though number of school is more in urban areas than the rural areas.

In this connection it may be mentioned that due weightage has to be given on the basis of population concentration and specially where the literacy rate is Very Low or Low. Keeping these two factors in mind, three sections of rural women has to be examined so that proper priority may be given in planning and implementation so as to make a positive change in the field of education.

In India, 22.25 per cent women are workers, the said percentages among the Scheduled Castes and Scheduled Tribes are 25.98 and 43.71, indicates that participation of ST women is more or less double the average percentage of the women workers. Here, it may be noted that in general the rural women folk constitutes 74.75 per cent of the total women population of India but their percentage of workers is only 18.57, i.e., less than one-fifth of the population.

On the other hand among the Scheduled Castes women 81.46 per cent live in rural areas and of them 22.03 are recognised as main workers which is also little less than one-fourth of their population. Only of the Scheduled Tribes females the percentage of working is about one-third of their population. It is true that, women folk and rural women in particular are yet to get opportunity to work specially in comparison to male population. Table 3.1 will help to get an overall view of the work force among the males and females.

Among the rural women 18.57 percent constitutes the workforce, which varies between 2.16 per cent (Punjab) to 42.03 per cent (Nagaland). There are 14 States/UTs where percentage of working population is above the percentage noted for India. Apart from main workers, there are 8.10 per cent workers, who are recognised as Marginal Workers (get employment below 181 days in a year). Of the three sections of women population, highest non-workers is present in Punjab with 95.63 per cent and lowest in Dadra & Nagar Haveli (48.95 per cent). Table 3.2 may be consulted for further details.

TABLE : 3.2

ALL INDIA RURAL FEMALE WORKFORCE : 1991 CENSUS

Sl. No.	STATE	Total Workers			Marginal Workers			Non-Workers		
		TOT POP (per cent)	SC (per cent)	ST (per cent)	TOT POP (per cent)	SC (per cent)	ST (per cent)	TOT POP (per cent)	SC (per cent)	ST (per cent)
01	Andhra Pradesh	36.96	47.63	45.99	5.52	4.84	6.60	57.52	47.53	47.42
02	Arunachal Pradesh	38.72	14.41	44.06	2.14	0.19	1.68	59.14	85.41	54.26
03	Assam	13.26	9.10	20.17	10.01	10.77	14.36	76.73	80.13	65.48
04	Bihar	10.79	19.90	22.85	5.47	4.85	16.44	83.74	75.25	60.71
05	Goa	18.53	26.58	29.27	5.39	6.59	-	76.08	66.83	70.73
06	Gujarat	17.70	19.99	26.37	17.90	14.82	22.97	64.40	65.19	50.66
07	Haryana	6.46	7.34	-	6.16	5.54	-	87.38	87.13	0.00
08	Himachal Pradesh	20.08	20.65	22.88	16.53	16.36	23.31	63.39	62.99	53.81
09	Karnataka	27.44	34.85	34.05	9.16	7.83	8.78	63.40	57.32	57.17
10	Kerala	13.35	28.17	29.53	3.52	5.39	7.60	83.14	66.43	62.86
11	Madhya Pradesh	26.93	29.98	33.35	12.34	10.68	16.26	60.74	59.34	50.39
12	Maharashtra	36.08	40.38	44.49	9.96	7.96	9.38	53.92	51.67	46.14
13	Manipur	37.20	21.10	45.54	6.01	10.92	2.85	56.78	67.98	51.61
14	Meghalaya	33.90	8.70	36.09	4.95	6.68	4.40	61.15	84.62	59.52
15	Mizoram	39.24	3.51	39.37	7.87	1.75	7.91	52.89	94.74	52.73

(Contd..)

(Contd..)

16 Nagaland	42.03	-	42.99	0.75	-	0.61	57.22	-	56.39
17 Orissa	12.83	15.74	23.36	9.79	8.90	17.54	77.38	75.36	59.10
18 Punjab	2.16	3.08	-	2.21	2.51	-	95.63	94.41	-
19 Rajasthan	15.26	16.47	18.18	17.99	16.82	23.64	66.75	66.71	58.19
20 Sikkim	29.61	26.77	30.29	1.87	1.38	1.73	68.53	71.85	67.98
21 Tamil Nadu	31.97	40.89	41.45	6.53	5.77	6.34	61.50	53.34	52.20
22 Tripura	10.40	6.09	18.85	4.18	3.12	6.61	85.42	90.79	74.54
23 Uttar Pradesh	8.36	12.64	19.71	5.81	6.30	14.12	85.84	81.06	66.18
24 West Bengal	8.74	9.76	34.18	4.33	4.36	8.07	86.93	85.88	57.75
UNION TERRITORIES									
01 Andaman & Nicobar Islands	7.61	-	11.56	6.75	-	16.16	85.64	-	72.27
02 Chandigarh	5.01	8.81	-	0.33	0.51	-	94.66	90.68	-
03 Dadra & Nagar Haveli	32.57	22.35	35.74	18.48	7.20	20.15	48.95	70.45	44.11
04 Daman & Diu	13.04	5.28	20.59	16.42	16.39	22.43	70.54	78.34	56.97
05 Delhi	4.84	7.68	-	0.62	0.72	-	94.54	91.59	-
06 Lakshadweep	5.42	-	5.26	1.54	-	1.57	93.04	-	93.17
07 Pondicherry	21.17	36.25	-	1.68	2.89	-	77.15	60.86	-
All India (Excluding J&K)	**18.57**	**22.03**	**30.95**	**8.10**	**6.99**	**14.55**	**73.32**	**70.98**	**54.50**

Out of total rural female workers, in India, majority are engaged as agricultural labourer (48.49 per cent) followed by cultivators (38.53 per cent). It is quite interesting to note that more than 2 per cent workers are engaged in tertiary sector like other than household industries, and other services. As per the data, about 90 per cent of the working population are still depend on agriculture and allied occupations. It is fact that occupational changes has also been noted among the rural women population but it is neither significant nor as expected, specially consulted after so many plan periods. In fact, they have every right to get the flavour of the development, which was a dream for them. For further details, Table 3.2 may be seen.

It has been discussed earlier that women in general and rural women in particular do not enjoy the status as the male do. It has also been stated that among the rural female, Scheduled Castes and Scheduled Tribes women have been able to make little progress though they are also engaged in different occupations along with their male counterpart.

In this regard, quite often it is stated that as majority of the women of these two sections of population are engaged in different economic pursuits so they are economically independent to a great extent or they have an economic status too. But this saying has no relation with the reality. In fact, just to have two square meals; they are to work hard. Thus, to understand the reality discussion has been made separately on Scheduled Castes and Scheduled Tribes rural women.

Working population of Rural women among the Scheduled Castes vary between 3.08 per cent (Punjab) to 47.68 per cent (Andhra Pradesh) and the average working force of this section of population in India is 22.03 per cent whereas it is only 11.13 per cent in urban areas.

There are only 10 States/UTs who have female workers more than 22.03 per cent noted for India. This also indicates that percentage of non—workers is also Very High, which vary between 53.34 per cent (Tamil Nadu) and 94.74 per cent (Mizoram). Apart from main workers a few percentage of female are recorded as marginal workers who work less than 181 days in a year. The lowest marginal worker is noted in Arunachal Pradesh with 0.19 per cent and highest in Rajasthan with 16.82 per cent of their total population.

Among the rural Scheduled Castes women workers, 71.10 per cent are engaged as agricultural labourers. More than 50 per cent agricultural workers are recorde in 13 states and in 6 states more than half of the women workers are engaged as cultivator. In India the average percentage of cultivators among the SC rural women is 19.18 per cent. Thus, it may be stated that more than 90 per cent of these workers are in agricultural sector.

Table 3.3 gives detailed about the occupational pattern of Scheduled Castes rural women which also indicates that very few women have taken up new avocations other than their primary occupation. Whatever small percentages of workers in other categories are recorded, amongst them mostly are unskilled labourers.

The Table further reveals that among the rural Scheduled Tribes women of India, 30.95 per cent are recorded as main workers, 14.55 per cent as marginal and 54.50 per cent as non-workers. Highest workers is observed in Andhra Pradesh with 45.99 per cent and lowest in Lakshadweep with 5.26 per cent. From the census it is also seen that percentage of tribal female workers is higher than women belong to other community. Most noteable observation is the participation of rural tribal women in cultivation, i.e., 48.60 per cent followed by agricultural labourer with 44.91 per cent. Thus, 93.51 per cent of the rural women of this section depend on agriculture sector. In 10 States and One UT, the said percentage of workers as cultivator has been noted between 54.97 (Tripura), 95.04 per cent (Arunachal Pradesh).

Here it may be noted that in most of the North Eastern States and in Himachal Pradesh, Rajasthan and UP, more tribal women are engaged as cultivator than as agricultural labourer. The highest agricultural labourer is recorded in Kerala with 63.81 per cent and lowest in Nagaland with 0.37 per cent.

This shows that diversification of occupation or occupational mobility is yet to take place in the economic life of the tribal women living in rural areas.

Considering these socio-economic information in the background, one will also agree that the concerned population i.e. rural women in general and Scheduled Caste and Scheduled Tribe in particular are lagging behind than their male counterpart in most of the spheres of life, mainly because of traditional cultural values. It is also true that the women crushed by the male dominated society, forgotten about their rights and status, their dues and honour, remembering only their responsibility and obligations required to be fulfilled by them by the society.

Development schemes, which are implementing through various Government and non-Government agencies are mainly given to male persons, though there are number of areas where female are more deserving. Mention may be made of : Rearing of livestock, cottage industry including Handicrafts, small business like tea shop, Grocery or Pan shop and/or small restaurants.

In view of this and keeping the data present in Table 3.3 it may be suggested that specific schemes are to be drawn on the bases of their participation in various occupational sectors so as the rural women of different States/UTs may not only get an opportunity but also may avail the same for their development.

Decentralisation of power has been made through three tier Panchayat system, in some states, women rather rural women are also empowered to participate in development programmes. If we see the lists of elected women members, will observe that total woman members are more than the seats reserved for them. This is surely a positive trend. But the question arises, How far they have been able to develop their ability for participating in the development programmes. Keeping their poor socioe—conomic background, whether they have been able to develop themselves for making the system a success.

It is true that through empowerment, rural women may develop themselves though there are some limitations, on the other hand if the concerned population, i.e., rural female folk can develop themselves, they can achieve their objective too.

Here, I like to quote Tagore's line,
Let her have the Strength to bear the Flag of Mission

Finally, I like to mention that unless women are developed, neither the family or society nor the country as a whole can make progress as desired or as expected.

Women or in other words the 'Mother' has to play a key role in the family, on whom the socialisation of the children depend. No children remain illiterate, if the mother is literate or educated. As the saying goes—"The hand that rocks the cradle, rules the world"

For achieving the proper status socio-economic development of the females particularly Scheduled Castes and Scheduled Tribes women should be given priority. Educational and employment opportunities, income generation schemes should be given to the women of all section. As women play the key role in the family this developmental schemes will be helpful to improve the overall socio-economic condition of the country.

Thus, if the women can achieve the right status in every corner of life, they will be able to achieve power, perform their duties and shoulder their responsibilities successfully.

TABLE : 3.3

DISTRIBUTION OF ALL INDIA RURAL FEMALE WORKFORCE IN SPECIFIC INDUSTRIAL CATEGORIES : 1991 CENSUS SELECTED CATEGORIES OF TOTAL WORKERS

	Cultivators			Agri. Labourers			Livestock		
Sl. No. State	*Tot Pop (per cent)*	*SC (per cent)*	*ST (per cent)*	*Tot Pop (per cent)*	*SC (per cent)*	*ST (per cent)*	*Tot Pop (per cent)*	*SC (per cent)*	*ST (per cent)*
01 Andhra Pradesh	24.49	8.72	33.48	63.73	86.99	59.62	0.67	0.33	1.33
02 Arunachal Pradesh	86.47	51.67	94.74	5.18	7.74	1.35	0.97	10.97	0.13
03 Assam	53.69	54.83	81.70	12.59	18.72	12.34	24.56	8.58	0.40
04 Bihar	32.93	9.64	58.08	61.22	86.27	36.44	0.18	0.14	0.22
05 Goa	29.98	4.80	0.00	21.79	17.89	16.67	2.92	0.90	0.00
06 Gujarat	35.17	10.56	37.17	50.56	75.93	57.08	6.43	2.09	0.60
07 Haryana	56.90	10.07	-	29.58	71.46	-	0.34	0.68	-
08 Himachal Pradesh	90.64	90.75	86.05	2.03	3.09	3.28	0.70	0.60	2.60
09 Karnataka	29.62	15.90	25.46	55.62	72.60	62.63	3.32	3.93	4.05
10 Kerala	6.53	2.05	12.03	42.25	63.16	63.81	7.56	9.90	12.65
11 Madhya Pradesh	54.88	35.27	57.31	39.26	55.59	39.57	0.44	0.25	0.46
12 Maharashtra	45.04	16.51	36.65	48.70	74.82	58.53	0.64	0.43	0.88
13 Manipur	73.71	59.36	92.67	8.97	13.78	2.72	0.48	0.33	0.09
14 Meghalaya	69.00	14.14	69.87	15.08	47.98	14.81	7.00	1.01	7.07
15 Mizoram	92.46	0.00	92.53	1.43	50.00	1.39	0.34	0.00	0.34

(Contd.)

(Contd..)

16 Nagaland	94.12	-	95.04	0.97		0.37	0.13	-	0.12
17 Orissa	27.59	12.25	32.19	57.85	68.41	59.15	0.71	1.00	0.67
18 Punjab	14.99	2.89	-	41.46	67.28	-	1.00	0.85	-
19 Rajasthan	74.52	58.64	69.91	19.27	32.20	26.01	1.36	1.01	1.17
20 Sikkim	75.67	72.78	75.43	7.73	9.59	4.27	1.36	2.06	1.31
21 Tamil Nadu	24.26	11.12	31.53	60.89	81.60	56.55	1.43	1.64	5.69
22 Tripura	43.11	20.21	54.97	34.70	37.20	37.06	5.15	10.50	2.25
23 Uttar Pradesh	52.77	32.54	73.45	38.61	59.97	13.73	0.44	0.59	0.57
24 West Bengal	19.86	12.69	21.39	45.89	63.86	61.81	7.09	2.72	11.26
UNION TERRITORIES									
01 Andaman & Nicobar Islands	23.79	-	0.00	5.62	-	0.00	7.77	-	8.22
02 Chandigarh	1.95	0.19	-	4.05	2.63	-	11.98	2.81	-
03 Dadra & Nagar Haveli	76.52	38.43	79.29	14.92	40.91	15.09	0.94	0.83	0.95
04 Daman & Diu	20.46	12.12	12.44	13.96	13.64	34.14	20.05	0.00	0.00
05 Delhi	9.14	0.90	-	10.81	12.26	-	0.68	0.39	-
06 Lakshadweep	0.00	-	0.00	0.00	-	0.00	19.33	-	20.35
07 Pondicherry	6.17	2.64	-	77.96	92.58	-	0.34	0.21	-
All India (Excluding J&K)	**38.93**	**19.18**	**48.60**	**48.49**	**71.10**	**44.91**	**2.14**	**1.36**	**1.72**

TABLE : 3.3 (Cont....)

DISTRIBUTION OF ALL INDIA RURAL FEMALE WORKFORCE IN SPECIFIC INDUSTRIAL CATEGORIES : 1991 CENSUS

	Selected Categories of Total Workers								
	Mining and Quarrying			*Household industries*			*Non-household industries*		
Sl. No. State	Tot Pop (per cent)	SC (per cent)	ST (per cent)	Tot Pop (per cent)	SC (per cent)	ST (per cent)	Tot Pop (per cent)	SC (per cent)	ST (per cent)
01 Andhra Pradesh	0.38	0.29	0.16	3.91	1.19	2.58	1.71	0.76	1.13
02 Arunachal Pradesh	0.00	0.00	0.00	0.14	0.00	0.13	0.48	0.65	0.19
03 Assam	0.08	0.010	0.02	1.99	6.68	1.01	0.80	2.05	0.43
04 Bihar	0.28	0.32	0.50	1.90	1.74	1.49	0.68	0.40	0.58
05 Goa	4.57	7.62	66.67	2.45	46.94	0.00	7.87	7.80	8.33
06 Gujarat	0.26	0.41	0.27	1.22	3.69	0.69	1.70	2.28	1.43
07 Haryana	0.04	0.11	-	1.00	1.06	-	3.50	7.83	-
08 Himachal Pradesh	0.01	0.01	0.01	0.70	1.38	1.00	0.77	1.10	0.86
09 Karnataka	0.44	0.94	0.45	1.46	1.52	1.29	5.02	2.40	3.39
10 Kerala	0.78	0.89	0.19	5.56	3.90	0.59	13.75	9.35	4.99
11 Madhya Pradesh	0.22	0.19	0.31	2.33	5.31	0.66	0.88	1.62	0.48
12 Maharashtra	0.14	0.12	0.21	1.17	3.38	0.66	1.24	1.86	1.11
13 Manipur	0.01	0.00	0.00	10.44	16.86	1.29	0.89	1.21	0.10
14 Meghalaya	0.24	0.00	0.22	0.42	0.03	0.37	0.30	1.52	0.28

(Contd..)

(Contd..)

15 Mizoram	0.00	0.00	0.00	0.21	0.00	0.21	0.04	0.00	0.04
16 Nagaland	0.00	-	0.00	0.41	-	0.38	0.22	-	0.19
17 Orissa	0.89	0.59	1.47	5.21	8.16	2.94	1.34	1.74	1.05
18 Punjab	0.00	0.00	-	3.43	3.43	-	6.44	7.91	-
19 Rajasthan	0.50	0.86	1.05	1.18	2.47	0.07	0.65	1.41	0.27
20 Sikkim	0.04	.011	0.01	0.30	0.29	0.65	1.53	3.55	2.18
21 Tamil Nadu	0.16	0.09	0.15	4.02	1.22	1.34	3.22	1.63	1.43
22 Tripura	0.07	0.04	0.00	2.63	6.56	0.05	1.72	3.47	0.73
23 Uttar Pradesh	0.06	0.15	0.04	2.43	1.98	7.71	1.58	1.39	1.73
24 West Bengal	0.21	0.26	0.31	11.84	7.27	1.72	6.91	4.95	2.23
UNION TERRITORIES									
01 Andaman & Nicobar Islands	1.85	-	0.00	15.35	-	72.30	2.01	-	0.00
02 Chandigarh	0.00	0.00	-	0.39	0.00	-	8.25	3.00	-
03 Dadra & Nagar Haveli	0.15	0.00	0.12	0.15	0.41	0.01	2.20	6.61	1.48
04 Daman & Diu	0.71	0.00	1.32	1.21	13.64	0.88	13.22	31.82	25.22
05 Delhi	4.36	0.97	-	1.87	0.79	-	20.35	34.84	-
06 Lakshadweep	0.00	-	0.00	1.83	-	1.95	15.00	-	15.75
07 Pondicherry	0.00	0.00	-	0.35	0.11	-	1.80	0.40	-
All India (Excluding J&K)	**0.28**	**0.32**	**0.39**	**2.91**	**2.71**	**1.17**	**2.30**	**1.92**	**0.96**

TABLE : 3.3 (Cont.)

DISTRIBUTION OF ALL INDIA RURAL FEMALE WORKFORCE IN SPECIFIC INDUSTRIAL CATEGORIES : 1991 CENSUS

Selected Categories of Total Workers

	Construction			Trade & Commerce			Transport & Storage			Other Services		
Sl. No. State	Tot Pop (per cent)	SC (per cent)	ST (per cent)	Tot Pop (per cent)	SC (per cent)	ST (per cent)	Tot Pop (per cent)	SC (per cent)	ST (per cent)	Tot Pop (per cent)	SC (per cent)	ST (per cent)
01 Andhra Pradesh	0.23	0.1	0.13	1.63	0.48	0.76	0.04	0.03	0.03	3.21	1.11	0.73
02 Arunachal Pradesh	1.25	7.74	0.42	0.53	1.29	0.40	0.03	0.00	0.02	4.96	20.00	2.62
03 Assam	0.07	0.10	0.03	0.62	2.11	0.25	0.08	0.18	0.04	5.53	6.64	3.78
04 Bihar	0.14	0.10	0.16	0.57	0.29	0.19	0.04	0.03	0.05	2.06	1.06	2.28
05 Goa	2.13	1.86	8.33	8.94	2.16	0.00	0.62	0.60	0.00	18.73	9.42	0.00
06 Gujarat	0.27	0.53	0.19	0.88	0.32	0.32	0.08	0.11	0.05	3.43	4.08	2.21
07 Haryana	0.75	1.95	-	0.53	0.42	-	0.09	0.09	-	7.26	6.33	-
08 Himachal Pradesh	0.58	0.36	1.35	0.31	0.25	0.60	0.08	0.04	0.06	4.19	2.41	4.19
09 Karnataka	0.26	0.53	0.13	1.47	0.65	1.04	0.06	0.05	0.03	2.72	1.18	1.53
10 Kerala	0.67	0.79	0.14	3.21	0.94	0.41	1.09	0.73	0.36	18.61	8.29	4.83
11 Madhya Pradesh	0.19	0.22	0.19	0.45	0.29	0.16	0.02	0.02	0.02	1.32	1.24	0.85
12 Maharashtra	0.31	0.34	0.29	0.73	0.40	0.57	0.04	0.05	0.03	2.00	2.10	1.06
13 Manipur	0.19	0.27	0.07	1.70	0.66	0.39	0.07	0.05	0.03	3.52	7.47	2.64
14 Meghalaya	0.42	0.00	0.14	2.66	13.64	2.60	0.07	0.00	0.07	4.82	18.69	4.56
15 Mizoram	0.07%	0.00%	0.07%	1.41%	0.00%	1.42%	0.02%	0.00%	0.02%	4.02%	50.00%	3.99%

(Contd..)

(Contd..)

16 Nagaland	0.19	-	0.18	0.32	-	0.27	0.04	-	0.03	3.60	-	3.40
17 Orissa	0.17	0.23	0.21	1.71	2.63	0.62	0.08	0.08	0.09	4.45	4.92	1.61
18 Punjab	0.80	0.77	-	2.38	1.75	-	0.32	0.20	-	29.17	14.92	-
19 Rajasthan	0.29	0.59	0.44	0.32	0.45	0.11	0.03	0.03	0.04	1.89	2.35	0.93
20 Sikkim	3.34	5.03	4.48	1.33	0.94	1.54	0.015	0.4	0.22	8.56	5.61	9.90
21 Tamil Nadu	0.27	0.15	0.14	1.17	0.34	0.72	0.08	0.04	0.05	4.49	2.16	2.40
22 Tripura	0.29	1.15	0.07	0.89	2.38	0.20	0.11	0.14	0.02	11.34	18.35	4.19
23 Uttar Pradesh	0.22	0.25	0.26	0.77	0.37	0.20	0.06	0.05	0.09	3.06	2.70	2.23
24 West Bengal	0.19	0.23	0.13	1.92	2.64	0.20	0.12	0.13	0.06	5.96	5.25	0.88
UNION TERRITORIES												
01 Andaman & Nicobar Islands	7.56	-	0.54	4.64	-	3.64	0.69	-	0.07	30.72	-	15.23
02 Chandigarh	7.16	5.82	-	8.95	7.32	-	0.62	0.56	-	56.65	77.67	-
03 Dadra & Nagar Haveli	1.08	4.13	0.78	0.51	0.83	0.23	0.58	0.00	0.63	2.96	7.85	1.43
04 Daman & Diu	8.07	0.00	12.33	13.66	1.52	4.52	0.68	0.00	0.00	7.98	27.27	9.14
05 Delhi	6.54	6.40	-	5.38	3.96	-	1.54	1.06	-	39.33	38.43	-
06 Lakshadweep	3.17	-	3.36	4.67	-	4.60	0.50	-	0.35	55.50	-	53.63
07 Pondicherry	0.22	0.09	-	5.25	1.10	-	0.01	0.00	-	7.88	2.87	-
All India (Excluding J&K)	**0.27**	**0.28**	**0.21**	**1.08**	**0.63**	**0.44**	**0.08**	**0.07**	**0.04**	**3.53**	**2.44**	**1.55**

2

Women in Text and Context : An Enquiry into Her Political and Economic Empowerment

Premanand Panda

Women in Text

In 1991 Women's World Submit Foundation was created with a mission to serve the implementation of women's and children's rights and the promised development goals adopted by the international community at UN submits and conferences and hold the leaders accountable to the promises made. It took birth as a follow up to the first world summit for children held in New York in 1990. Till date there have been four Women's World Submit Foundation has sat for four times. Each sitting had come up with new set of strategies to liberate women from all types of bandages.

With regard to status of women, irrespective of developed and developing nations, there is no dearth of research articles and books in the areas of status, role development, education, employment, political participation, health, organisational agencies, gender studies, studies on social problems, attitudinal studies, rights (Legal and Cultural) and equality with men in socio-economic and demographic representation, criminological issues, role of women in advertisement, marketing and management, NGO Sector and women participation, tribal and rural women, changing aspects of women in social economic and cultural context, etc. and even as she is projected in romance, literature, struggle and movements and so on. In India there are more than some hundred studies in diverse fields both theoretical and empiric frontiers. However, majority works are being undertaken by the male researchers and since recently a few women social scientists have started their enquiry on women problem.

Before we go to scan how the women as a persons have been projected in texts let us first browse them through the events of field experiences of a few known female anthropologists. In fact, male and female anthropologists whom contributed substantial to the field of knowledge stand in different relationships to their respective gender groups (Ellen 1984 : 119). Further, it has been reported that early female anthropologists were mainly remained unmarried, single and tough *(ibid.)*. They were considered vulnerable to certain types of field situation and therefore they had their attention to topics thought to be less problematic and particularly suitable to them. This can be seen from the diary of Mead who reacted to Boa's direction to take up the task of studying adolescents in south seas (Mead 1977 : 19). British female anthropologist, the research student of A.R. Radcliffe-Brown, who advised Miss Powdermaker to take a gun along with her as a precaution while working in Lesu. The lady student of American ethnologist Prof. Franz Boas, Ruth Benedict had to bribe a girl to sleep alongside her while she was working among the primitive people (Mead 1959:299). Rosemary had to select the field where her husband was working so that she may avoid any unwanted situation (Ellen 1984). Indian female field worker carried out her field under the protection of her father-in-law while working among the Gond people (1975). Ellen writes that although there are a few female social anthropologist who had remarkable influence on the subject, they were never remain occupants of the departmental academic posts (1984). The first enlightened educated lady scooter rider of Pune Dr I. Karve who was supposes to had a feeling equipotent with man had dedicated her book to her husband's lotus feet. This gives us an idea that the female irrespective of position including the female social anthropologists were apprehensive when remain out of home and were remained under the male ideological influence. Referring to the working condition of a few female anthropologists including Lona

Mayer who worked among the Gusii during late 1940s Ellen has stated that women studies women centred problems have opened a new chapter on the changes in social and moral consciousness in the researchers' societies which have been influenced by the resurgence of feminism (1984:120).

Feminist perspectives on women have projected a new angle of vision at the intellectual discourse. This in spirit, content and approach oppose male world and hence an antipodal to male chauvinism The feminist perspective intends to liberate the women from all forms of bondages and hither to imposed subhuman statuses. One effect ot the feminist movement has been an increase in sociological studies directed specifically at the roles of women in society in general and in the family and marriage in particular. The American sociologist Jessie Bernard, for instance, argued that the study of marriage must focus both on husbands' and on wives' expectations and achievements. She noted that married men are generally more successful than single men in achieving their goals in life, whereas the opposite is true for modern married and unmarried women. This view contradicts that of Young and Willmott, who saw the modern symmetrical family as a step toward greater equality and similarity of roles between husband and wife. Much of the data Bernard cited was psychological. American wives are known to be much more prone to anxiety and depression than their husbands, and this, she argued, reflects the unfairness in marital roles as conceived in American society.

Ann Oakley a feminist from Britain had examined the changing roles of women since the Industrial Revolution and, in particular, the emergence of a new status of woman as housewife. Oakley, and many others in feminist circles, have regarded the role of housewife as degrading to women in that it prevents them from achieving economic and social independence on the same basis as men. Feminist movements at the global level and more specifically among the developed nations have been committed to the achievement for women of full legal, political, social, economic, educational and employment equality with men.

This angle of vision of functionalists who argued that in favour of statuesque and the division of labour in family as part of functional necessity and mutual contribution of members of family for maintenance of harmonic ordered relationships among members. They offer explanations for the role of women as mother, wife, sister, daughter and other in-law to those who tagged to the family through marital links within the family in managing the human and non-human resources, peer and co-worker and neighbour in the community set-up contributing towards the harmonic order of socio-cultural transactions. The changes come into force at the enactment and expectation of role of women are viewed as a response to the externalities. The functionalist normally gives importance to the essential elements that ensure the survival of the social processes.

Irrespective of oriental, and modern capitalistic societies one of the effects of the feminist movement has been a greater awareness in society as a whole. It views a double standard in sexual behaviour and a growing feeling that such a standard is unfair to women. Under this cultural code of conduct it is permissible for men to engage in premarital and, to some extent, even extramarital sexual intercourse, while women are expected to remain chaste before marriage and faithful to their husbands afterward. This double stadard and its inherent assumption of sexual inequality is a cause of concern for many women. Marxist interpretation indicate that the women are the reserve army of labour and the women have been truncated to assume their equal rights at par with men due to the existing male dominated ideological construct. To get out of that and come to the concrete terms some sort of counter ideological approach is mandatory. It is stated by a few that economic independence will lead to social independence. To be an actor in the power game is to hope for opportunity to progress. Women in order to assume equal power like that of men need to get into decision making body in some form or other. However, raising voice to be heard around for political gain does not have smooth route rather the male power would not only oppose but take steps to see that the possible areas of entry to resources get plug.

With regard to the political rights even in western society the right of women by law to vote in national and local elections was denied till recently. Texts have revealed that women were excluded from voting in ancient Greece and Republican Rome, as well as in the few democracies that had emerged in Europe by the end of the 18th century. When the franchise was widened, as it was in the United Kingdom in 1932, women continued to be denied all voting rights. The constant struggle against the male chauvinism and strategies adopted in favour of women franchise through writing, press conferences, meetings made the ruling parties agreeable to the terms and conditions laid down by the women leaders. The question of women's voting rights finally became an issue in the 19th century, and the struggle for political freedom was particularly intense in Great Britain and the United States during the later half of 19th and early half of the 20th century. However, it was slightly different in some of the western nations. By the early years of the 20th century, women had won the right to vote in national elections in New Zealand (1893), Australia (1902), Finland (1906), and Norway (1913). In Sweden and the United States they had voting rights in some local elections.

World War I and its aftermath speeded up the enfranchisement of women in the countries western world. Before 1930s women in 28 additional countries acquired equal voting rights with men in national elections. These countries included Soviet Russia (1917); Canada (1918); Germany, Austria, Poland, and Czechoslovakia (1919); the United States and Hungary (1920); Great Britain (1928); Burma (now Myanmar; 1922); Ecuador (1929); South Africa (1930); Brazil, Uruguay, and Thailand (1932); Turkey and Cuba (1934); and the Philippines (1937). In a number of these countries, women were initially granted the right to vote in local self governments like municipal or other local bodies and in few cases perhaps in provincial elections. Only later were they granted the vote in national elections.

Immediately after World War II, France, Italy, Romania, Yugoslavia, and China had thought of allowing women to exercise their franchise. Full suffrage for women was introduced in India by the constitution two years after independence in 1949; in Pakistan women received full voting rights in national elections in 1956. In another decade the total number of countries that had given women the right to vote had reached more than 100, partly because nearly all countries that gained independence after World War II guaranteed equal voting rights to men and women in their constitutions. By 1971 Switzerland allowed women to vote in federal elections. In 1973 women were granted full voting rights in Syria. Even now Women continue to be denied voting rights in many of the conservative Arab countries bordering the Persian Gulf. The United Nations Convention on the Political Rights of Women, adopted in 1952, provides that women shall be entitled to vote in all elections on equal terms with men, without any discrimination.

In Great Britain woman suffrage was first advocated by Mary Wollstonecraft in her book *A Vindication of the Rights of Woman* (1792) and was demanded by the Chartist movement of the 1840s. The demand for woman suffrage was increasingly taken up by prominent liberal intellectuals in England from the 1850s on, notably by John Stuart Mill and his wife, Harriet. The first woman suffrage committee was formed in Manchester in 1865, and 1867 Mill presented to Parliament this society's petition. This demanded the vote for women and contained about 1,550 signatures. The Reform Bill of 1867 contained no provision for woman suffrage, but meanwhile woman suffrage societies were forming in most of the major cities of Britain, and in the 1870s these organizations submitted to Parliament petitions demanding the franchise for women and containing a total of almost three million signatures.

In west the right to vote in parliamentary elections in USA was still denied to women, however, despite the considerable support that existed in Parliament for legislation to that effect. In 1897 the various suffragist societies united into one National Union of Women's Suffrage Societies, thus bringing a greater degree of coherence and organization to the movement. Out of frustration at the lack of governmental action, however, a segment of the woman suffrage movement became more militant under the leadership of Emmeline Pinehurst and her daughter Cristobel. After the return to power of the Liberal Party in 1906, the succeeding years saw the defeat of seven suffrage bills in Parliament. As a consequence, many suffragists became involved in increasingly violent actions as time went on. These women militants, or suffragettes, as they were known, were sent to prison and continued their protests there by engaging in hunger strikes. Meanwhile, public support of the woman suffrage movement grew in volume, and public demonstrations, exhibitions, and processions were organized in support of women's right to vote. When World War I began, the woman suffrage organizations shifted their energies to aiding the war effort, and their effectiveness did much to win the public wholeheartedly to the cause of woman suffrage. The need for the enfranchisement of women was finally recognized by most members of Parliament from all three major parties, and the resulting Representation of the People Act was passed by the House of Commons in June 1917 and by the House of Lords in February 1918. Under this act, all women age 30 or over received the complete franchise. An act to enable women to sit in the House of Commons was enacted shortly afterward. In 1928 the voting age for women was lowered to 21 to place women voters on an equal footing with male voters.

From the founding of the United States, women were almost universally excluded from voting. Only when women began to chafe at this restriction, however, was their exclusion made explicit. The movement for woman suffrage started in the early 19th century during the agitation against slavery. Women such as Lucretia Mott showed a keen interest in the antislavery movement and proved to be admirable public speakers. When Elizabeth Cady Stanton joined the antislavery forces, she and Mott agreed that the rights of women, as well as those of slaves, needed redress. In July 1848 they issued a call for a convention to discuss the issue of women's rights; this convention met in Stanton's hometown, Seneca Falls, New York, on July 19-20, 1848, and issued a declaration that called for woman suffrage and for the right of women to educational and employment opportunities. It was followed in 1850 by the first national convention of the women's movement, held in Worcester, Massachusetts, by Lucy Stone and a group of prominent Eastern suffragists. Another convention, held in Syracuse, New York, in 1852, was the occasion of the first joint venture between Stanton and the dynamic suffragist leader Susan B. Anthony; together these two figures led the American suffragist movement for the next 50 years *(Encyclopaedia Britania 2001).*

Other woman suffrage conventions were held as the movement gained its first mass strength, but at first no way of extending the vote to women was known except by amendments to the constitutions of the various states. Several attempts were made in this regard after the American Civil War (1861-65), but even though the Territory of Wyoming granted women the right to vote in all elections in 1869, it soon became apparent that an amendment of the federal Constitution would be a preferable plan. Accordingly, the National Woman Suffrage Association was formed in 1869 with the declared object of securing the ballot for women by an amendment to the Constitution. Anthony and Stanton were the leaders of his organization, which held a convention every year for 50 years after its founding. In 1859 another organization, the American Woman Suffrage Association, was founded by Lucy Stone with the aim of securing woman suffrage by obtaining amendments to that effect in the constitutions of the various states. In 1890 the two organizations united under the name National American Woman Suffrage Association and worked together for almost 30 years.

When Wyoming entered the Union in 1890, it became the first state whose constitution accorded women the right to vote. Subsequently, vigorous campaigns were conducted to persuade state legislatures to submit to their voters amendments to state constitutions conferring full suffrage to women in state affairs. Efforts were also made to give women the right to vote in presidential elections and, in some states, the right to vote in municipal and local elections. In the next 25 years various individual states yielded to the movement's demands and enfranchised their women; each such state increased the members of Congress elected partly by women. These members were thus at least partly obliged by the nature of their constituency to vote for a woman suffrage amendment to the United States Constitution. By 1918 women had acquired equal suffrage with men in 15 States.

World War I, and the major role played in it by women in various capacities, broke down most of the remaining opposition to woman suffrage in the United States. Amendments to the federal Constitution concerning woman suffrage had been introduced into Congress in 1878 and 1914, but the 1878 amendment had been overwhelmingly defeated, and the 1914 amendment had narrowly failed to gain even a simple majority of the votes in the House of Representatives and the Senate (a two-thirds majority vote in Congress was needed for the amendment to be sent to the state legislatures for ratification). By 1918, however, both major political parties were committed to woman suffrage, and the amendment was carried by the necessary two-thirds majorities in both the House and Senate in January 1918 and June 1919, respectively. Vigorous campaigns were then waged to secure ratification of the amendment by two-thirds of the state legislatures, and on August 18, 1920, Tennessee became the 36th state to ratify the amendment. On August 26 the Nineteenth Amendment was proclaimed by the secretary of state as being part of the Constitution of the United States. Women in the United States were enfranchised on an equal basis with men.

The right of citizens of the United States to vote shall not be denied or abridged by the United States or by any State on account of sex. Although it is a free country yet the non-native, who recently acquired citizenship and the Negroes have not been given equal rights in practice. Being liberated from the colonial clutches of British empire in 1947, women in India have achieved voting right at all levels almost three years prior to the American women. To help the preferential discriminated category of people in India, i.e., women, the parliamentarians have successfully took many pleas to avoid any discussion of their reservation issue and the said issue yet remained unsolved. Historically, the United Kingdom and the United

States provide characteristic examples of the struggle for woman suffrage in the 19th and 20th centuries and got benefits and in India it had not made much headways, however, marginally it is gaining strength.

In the recent twelve-day long international conference held at Beijing, China the violence against women, reproductive rights of women, status of her health and factors responsible for it and many other diverse field of urgent relevance across the political boundary of the nations were the major concern. Realising the disparities in developing and developed countries the conference urged to enact and enforce legislation to guarantee the rights of women and men to equal for equal work, extend social security and adopt and implement laws against the exploitation, discrimination based on sex and labour.

Section Two

The ancient scripts on palm leaf, copper plates, stone crafts, wooden engravings, terracotta and images of different postures depicted in monuments evoke memories of the Indians on events of his appreciation, perception and motifs on women. The present political geography of India was parts of the small and big principalities where the cultures were different in forms and contents. Ethnic markers were distinct and the material culture traits were ecologically determined. The rare commodities available in association with the monuments in the different geographical locations revealing the cultural relics of remote history offer ritual explanations. It has been stated by a good number of archaeologists and anthropologists that during the halcyon days of Vedic era women were honoured as creators and preservers of Indian race, pride, dignity and status. Further it is repeated by many that no sacred events, no ceremony was deemed sacrosanct unless and until the female as *grihini, jaya, sahadharmini* and *sahadharmini* took part in its proceedings. Her role was indispensable and integral to the function of vital rituals and socio-cultural transactions. The post-Vedic era and more specifically in Brahminical era when the concept of pollution and purity associated with occupation assumed the sharp distinction between the worth and status of occupation and occupational specialists, the women became the subject of humiliation. This is how in earlier Aryan cultural phase she was the first victim.

Many number of Vedas, Upanishadha, Brahminical and Buddhist assertions mentioned the equality of status between men and women during ancient India. The woman has been referred to as Bramhacharini, Brahmhabadini, and mentioned the names of great scholars like Gargi, Vachaknavi, Maitreyi. In Srautra and Grihasutras it is mentioned that the wife and husband are co-partners in important religious ceremonies as complementary to each other.

In IX the chapter of *Manu Sanhita* and *Manu Smruti* the status of the women has been discriminately indicated wherein it has been viewed from patriarch angle and therefore represented as low. A few Sanskrit slokas may be cited in order to locte the way the women status has been evaluated in texts. For example, the aforesaid scripts depicted that

Pita rakhsati kaumare bharta rakshati jwaubane
Raskhati stabare putra na stree swatantramaharti

This means, the female is never worth liberated and hence at the childhood she is kept guarded by father, during youth remains under the protection of husband and during the old age protected and taken cared of by the son. That her feeling of insecurity in our ancient time and her dependency on male members at all time reflect in another verse as stated below :

Ne kashti jositah saktahprashahya parirakshitam
Yeterupayajogostu saktastah parirakshitum

Manu in his scripts further stated that while offering security the women they need to be controlled due to the fact that they have been possessing powerful vices. Befitting to that similarly, it is stated that no female can be controlled by force. They can only be controlled by tricks and tactical moves.

Pano durjanasansargah patya cha barahoatanam
Swapneanograhabasascha narinam dusanani satt

There are six vices of woman and these are : liquor habit, unscrupulous friendship, staying away from husband, aimlessly moving here and there, un-time sleep and living with outsiders. In certain context Manu has equated women even with the material goods and the domesticated animals. Male and female distinction at the sphere of control, ownership, entry to and use of resources were extremely sharp. The women were comparable to the sub-humans and material goods—a commodity like that alienated from humanity. It added further menace to her wounded status during the Muslim rule and then she was almost reduced to the status of chattel. She was the object of oblivion then. In the great traditions like Mahabharat, Ramayan, Upanisadhs the women have been projected as subordinate to men. The history of the social institution can be reconstructed taking evidences from the contemporary tribal society.

In all known matriarchal tribal communities the right to property, decisive power for vital issues in family and community, directive and monitoring roles for almost all socio-economic transactions and such other powers provide evidences to suggest that women enjoy better status. There are widely known theories on the origin and development of social institutions referring to matri-centric family as ealier to the patri-centric ones. This, however, apparently opposes universal principle of kinship indicating that male exercises power over female irrespective of any type of societies. Female as the inventor of plant domestication and crop cultivation had receded back to the hands of male power with the emergence of private property rights and decline of community property rights. Female infanticide as a part of institution came up quite late and was rationalised as a necessity during the post-Vedic period. Although it is an un-denying fact that she is genetically powerful, she has been systematically marginalised in socio-cultural frontiers. The raw data on a few biosocial markers would take us to the reality of gender discrimination.

In west with the Industrial Revolution the work situation changed for both men and women. In India it has not made any headway to liberate the women from the male subjugation. Even today the hearth and home remained the centre of production and family life in developed countries. It is indicate that Indian women enjoy better legal rights compared to a few other countries. The Hindu Code Bill referring to the equal inheritance rights 1956, the Anti Dowry Act 1961 amended in 1984 and 1986, equal pay requirement 1976, Prohibition of Sati, and many legislations in favour of women seen mentioned under socio-economic crimes probably contributed to truncate the women movements. The human rights and fundamental rights provide many more provisions to protect human dignity and honour. All these provisions and legal supports have meaning only then they have public acclaim.

With industrialization the factory became the workplace and the town the dwelling place. However, for society like ours the urbanisation has slowly opened the doors for women emancipation and provided scope to peep out side. Education has contributed for their entry to jobs in formal organisations. The informal sector still encourages her for employing women due to cheap labour cost. The role of women in the family and workforce did not change much.

Till recently the role of the male was considered as the bread winner and security provider. With women relegated to household and domestic tasks. This was caused, perhaps, not so much by the change from farming to industrial technology as by a growing humanitarian protest against the harsh treatment of women and children in the early factory system. Legislation—most notably in Britain and in India—raised the minimum age for child labour in factories, set limits on the working hours of women and children, and barred them from certain dangerous and heavy hazardous occupations. Thus, more women were engaged primarily in domestic tasks and child care at home while the men went out to work. Being the sole wage earner in the family it reinforced the man's traditional position as the head of the family, who was expected to direct the lives of his dependents. By and large irrespective of families with earning females the families remain as patriarchal. Whatever authority the woman exercised derived from her status as mistress of the household.

The tradition of the deferential female wedded to motherhood and domesticity persisted throughout last few centuries. After the coming of electric power near the close of the 19th century, advances in technology brought labour-saving devices such as washing machines and vacuum cleaners into the home the urban women could see some changes. Although they changed the nature of some tasks and freed the housewife from some drudgery, they did little to lessen the amount of time she spent on household duties. In a sense to bring a washing machine means to reduce expenditure and use services of the housewife in a mechanised way.

At the same time that women's household work was being transformed by technology, changes were occurring in the economy and society leading to the growth of administrative and service jobs. The extension of public education created a demand for more teachers, and growing industrial and commercial enterprises required more office workers and sales people. While men could have and earlier had performed teaching and clerical tasks, it was discovered that it was cheaper to hire women for these occupations. The prevailing attitude was that, since men were the heads of households, they had to be paid enough to support a family. In west most women who entered the work force in the United States before World War II were single and did not have families to support; hence, they could be paid lower wages. In India the preference to pay more to male than female for similar work is continuing. This inequality in men's and women's pay scales, even for equal work, still prevails in United States as we maintain the wage difference for male and female.

Technological changes affecting the maternal role of women also had an impact on their ability to leave the home. The development of contraceptive devices and the baby bottle and rubber nipple gave women greater freedom, making it easier for them to take outside jobs. This is the case in urban sector, in rural the children are kept at the care of the elder daughter or with the old parents to let her participate in the labour market to maintain family. Even if her employment was interrupted by childbirth, the woman use to take the child to the work spot to feed the baby periodically and join the work effectively.

Many working women performed tasks closely related to their traditional household work. When clothes were less often made at home but purchased readymade at stores, for example, women were hired as seamstresses in the clothing industry. Even after national emergencies such as the world wars, during which women were encouraged to take manufacturing jobs to replace the men who were in military service, women returned to housekeeping or to traditionally female occupations such as office work and nursing.

In the 1970s married women began entering the labour force in great numbers, and the strict segregation of women into certain occupations began to lessen somewhat as new opportunities arose for female workers in traditionally male occupations. New technology has meant that many tasks that once required heavy physical exertion, and hence were restricted to men, can now be performed simply by pushing buttons. Operating a bulldozer, for instance, does not need muscle power so much as alertness, judgment, and coordination-qualities as plentiful in women as in men. Nevertheless, the entrance of women into occupations formerly the province of men proved to be slower than expected. There are works prerogative of male and also a few of females with the change the counterpart normally chide and look down upon. This persistent occupational segregation by sex is largely responsible for sizable differences in rates of pay that still exist. It would appear that, although rapid technological progress has enabled women in highly industrialized nations to cast off certain traditional roles, technological determinism or technological rationality does not always reign over cultural views and social practices handed down from the past. Housing industry, home industry (like lace making, garment, pickle and *papad* making), poultry and terracotta industry have encouraged since recently. In housing industry the women masons to participate in cement works which was hither to remained a prerogative of male created intolerable compromise with the male workers. To do this, with the help of a few non-government agencies, they had to face problems at home and also outside. However, their constant perseverance made them enter the job and overcome the difficulties.

Status of women at the international level among the comparable countries may be seen to evaluate the relative position of our womenfolk. For example, the life expectancy (1992), for India, Pakistan and Brazil were 59.9, 58.3 and 68.7 respectively. India is only one of the four countries where the total number of males is more than the females. The sex ratio that was 970 in 1901; 946 in 1941 was reduced to 935 per 100 male in 1981. The sex ratio has changed to 927 female per 1000 male in 1991. This has been attributed to the perpetual social preference for male child. The selective female mortality from the infanticide onwards has been a known phenomenon. The life expectancy between male and female also show the earlier death of female. The fact is not entirely related to the economic status. The frequent use of technique of amniocentesis under the pretext of determining the high risk of abnormal foetuses and to identify the sex of unborn and terminating the pregnancy substantially contribute the existing sex ratio. In our nation 45.7 per cent of agricultural work is being done by women and the girl child under 15 years who form 20 per cent of country's population share 20 per cent of burden. At the national level as per 2001 census the male literacy 75.83 female literacy 54.16.

According to religious and philosophical thought, the women is supreme power. She has been referred to as *sakti*, the source of energy. She is the goddess Durga, Kali, Chandi, and Sabitri. These features are attributed to her for different moods she is in. She can create, destroy and protect and a man in Hindu pantheon is never complete without her. The Hindu idea of God as half male and half female is bisexual. She has no identity without a husband. She assumes the blessing from the elders as *saubhagyavati* (the fortunate) only after marriage. In Indian context, no Hindu family tolerate her deviation from the code of conduct for a married woman. She needs to be *pativrata* refers to total devotion to the husband. Therefore gods are worshipped with their consorts. The deities like Narayan and Shiva are worshipped along with Lakshmi and Parvati respectively.

The status of Draupadi as a common wife of Pandavas have been critically viewed by Prativa Roy in her epoch-making book the *Jaynaseni* where she has clearly stated Draupadi's unwilling acceptance to the desire of all the husbands and who could do no support in the Kaurava Maha Sabha where she had to surrounded herself to another powerful male the Krishna. No Pandavas ever stretched their hands to take Draupadi to heaven while they walked towards paradise. In Ramayana, Sita—the wife of Rama—had to under- go test of *Agniparikshya* (a trial before public) to prove her chastity for no fault to her. She had to tolerate.

The little girls in the traditional patriarchal family are being socialized to the social expectations such as tolerant, docile, bowing head, walking no upright serving seniors and juniors it would be clear if the feeling of a girl child is mentioned here: 'Oh God, please make me a boy in my next life' (Mohanti 1973:80). The movement of a girl after attaining puberty gets severely restricted and kept under strict control of the mother and grandmother in the family. Upright walking viewed low and spoof with the simile of mare walk. They are not expected to laugh loud, talk in high pitch, run in front of others presence. Soft speaking polite and affectionate approach are viewed as valued ingredient for a women. Like that a women who cannot produce children is considered inauspicious. A married woman gains her place in her husband's house when she becomes a mother. It gives her confidence and a feeling of 'security'. Invariably her duty is not over until she is blesses with a son. If she is unable to produce one she is blamed and no blames to husband. When a child is born to a rural wife the first question people ask is, Is it a son? In ritual dimension the male is given importance over female as are being observed in the festival like Rakhi, Karvachauth, Bhaijayintia, Puajayintia where sister wish for long life and prosperity of brother, wife worship for the all round development of husband, sisters observe ritual for brother as is being practised in western part of Orissa and married women and mothers worship deity to derive leasing for long life of the sons respectively. In rural society there are numerous riddles referring to the low status of the women. For example,

Mrs. Sudevi Panda aged around 84 of Berhampur of Ganjam district on request spoke out a few riddles of her natal village current during her childhood period. One of the riddle says as follows:

Mai marana pita tuna jete male sete guna

This means that the life of the female in society is comparable to that of the bitter curry and therefore the more they die the better for the society. The second riddle says like this :

Andira jara badhi baigana besara kara
maikina jara dharad dharda paiti kara

This means that when a male suffers from fever it is necessary to prepare therapeutic food for quick recovery and for female to get rid of the suffering she needs to put hard labour. Such are the perception of women on women a few decades back. In her opinion the birth of daughters in upper caste middle class family is a big liability. It is liability because of the dowry in marriage and the investment on daughters for education goes to benefit the in-law house provided the husband permits them to take jobs. At times higher education of the girl costs the parents to pay heavy dowry during the daughter's marriage.

Section Three

Women in Context

There are huge references on girl child menace and the women marginalisation. It is viewed that empowering women and raising status of women can be done through the integrated approach involving legislation, attitudinal changes, providing women greater access to resources, education, skill and knowledge. However, the mere visible economic independence such as representation in employment scenario, participation in production process and earning appropriate worth of labour will not change the status so long they are disallowed to dispose off the family property almost equal to men and take effective role in the decision making process in all vital family issues. To help changing the women status it is necessary that the male and the female must change their attitude. In a recent study, it was seen that male attitude toward the female even among the educated have not changed much (Panda *et al* 1988-89). In independent India there are almost thirty-eight articles of the Constitution mention about the safeguards, provisions to emancipate them in all frontiers yet the status has not changed much. In fact any law is powerful only when they have public supports and bolstered by resourceful enforcement.

There are helpless widows who earn their livelihood from within the village resources and mostly by the mercy of the rich gentries. The young widows have to carry blames for no faults of their. Sexual harassments are not unknown and there is hardly any support to them from the family and relatives in case of being victim of such exploitation. Widow marriage has seldom implemented. The devadashis are sexually exploited in the name of God. Some of them are the hangovers of the feudal tradition in India. The same attitude continue to a great extent even now although due to the impact of modernisation, rise in literacy level, increase of awareness changes are marked in semi-urban and urban areas. However the educated working women even now are expected to honour the oppressive traditions and not to cross the expectation of patriarch norms.

In known history, agriculture has been the chief human occupation, and heavy physical labour was not confined to men. Women performed backbreaking chores like grinding grain by hand in a stone quern, drawing and carrying water from stream and river or pulling from deep well, gathering fuel wood, and, feeding children, old dependents and cattle, churning milk to make butter. In India almost all societies perhaps the only period when women were given a respite was immediately before and after giving birth. She was expected of maintaining balanced human relations while not displeasing any inside and outside the house. Women like Sarojini Naidu, Indira Gandhi, Ramabai Ranade, Iravati Karve, Kiran Bedi, Geeta Mehta, Brinda Karat, Medha Patkar cannot be taken as examples to tell that the status of women in India has gone up. These great ladies are not Indian women rather they ae the daughters of India. To be more specific the women at grassroots are the Indian women. In real sense, she is defenceless, marginalised and subjugated although they constitute almost half the population. Now question comes what to do and how to improve the status of women? One of the strategies adopted by women folk in rural India to empower themselves was the formation of self help groups and go for small cooperative mode. In fact, empowerment entails two things; one that concerned with neighbourhood committee ensuring that with their association the people are provided with equal opportunities for basic necessities and scope for socio-economic advancement such that the people in question will be capable of adopting to the demanding new situations and the second; people making themselves heard in wider decision making arena and generate fertile ground for power decentralisation to participate and enjoy the available services and meet their needs without discrimination. A few NGOs acted as facilitators in this venture.

From Hyderabad experience it has been realised that women can do meaningful contribution for themselves, and for their families with all dignity and pride through the cooperative movement. In fact they fought and achieved what their counterparts in urban areas could only wish to match. From the case studies reported it has been ascertained that women's cooperatives foster community initiatives facilitating decision making through democratic processes. Orissa Government had also took steps to create new employment opportunities for the women since with five year plan period and through development agencies extended the financial help and imparted training inputs to the women of rural and tribal economically weaker section. The immediate effect of this development schemes were the extra pressure on women. They had to play dual role as producers and home makers.

In many areas women are seen employed themselves in *biri* making where in some one supplies the raw materials and they were asked to roll the *biri* bundles as finished products. The employers supply thread, tobacco, and tendu leaves and a conical small metal rod. The colour of the thread differentiate the owners. For each bundle the women were given fixed wage. The second variety of employment was in plucking up tendu leaves, collecting mahua flowers, chaar seeds, genduli gums, broom sticks, barks, collecting honey, collecting tubers, roots and shoots and other forest products a portion of which they sell to the merchant or in the local market to meet the other essential needs. The third variety of engagement is the employment in home industries such as looms for weaving, bamboo crafts for basket making and the like. In many cases they buy the law materials and at home prepare the finish products to sell in the market. Some scholars have highlighted a few characteristics of women employment which can be put in three broad categories namely:

(a) Employment as an extension to the household activities like poultry, food processing (pickle, spice, masala papad, etc), and family tradition based on crafts (zari works, metal, stone and wood engraving, and embroidery, etc).

(b) Making use of acquired skill to meet the market demands (biri making, match stick preparation, etc.

(c) Retail trading on the garments, flower decorative, meal and tiffin packets and their preparation and supply to the floating population, preparing puffed rice sweets dolls, etc.

Here is a case where one NGO (Manav Adhikar Seva Saminiti— the MASS) figured as outside help giver in form of initiator, facilitator, negotiator and consultant for the people at the grassroots. The objective here is that by self employment there will be a greater freedom for persons to select the occupation in which she hope for a change in the quality of life. At the initial meeting organised by MASS the people has lot many questions in head:

Whether a poor whose tomorrow is uncertain and today is conditioned by labour market that can employ him can go for some saving for future?

Can poor female folks drawn from different ethnic background join together to form some informal groups to protect their common interest?

Can they create a bank for them to support themselves in advancing their skills and meet exigencies so that they can have a say in the decision making processes and gradually participate in development activities? and can it organised in inter village level? and so on.

Role of MASS

The operational area for the MASS for the purpose of micro credit is rural and tribal villages of Sambalpur district. The case referred here is the SSG (Small Saving Group) operating in 36 villages distributed over two Blocks namely: Jujumara and Rengali of Sambalpur district, Orissa. Each village has got one SSG. In each SSG there are at least eight members. There are about 486 beneficiaries enrolled. The members of the voluntary organisation had organised several meetings in the villages informally before they motivate the village female folk to go for the formation of self-help groups. They had organised street dramas, and composed a few songs in the traditionally known popular tune and rhythms so that people at the grassroots can remember and internalise easily. The hierarchy of needs of the people in general and the females in particular were ascertained through the peoples participatory research designs using many unconventional techniques. The informal groups were formed in those villages with their informal leaders drawn from among the upper middle age category. The members of the MASS did not impose their own choice at any point of time during the formation of the self-help groups, they rather offered alternatives so that the local cultural norms do not violate and interacting female groups can be formed. After the establishment of good rapport with the village female folk and thorough persuasion of the lady volunteers in favour of the poor housewives the villagers generated a hope of self-confidence to escape from the clutch of the village evils such as saukars, liquor vendors, etc. This voluntary organisation where the author's is the president had started the SSG with an investment of Rs.5000 for five villages. Each village was given Rs. 1000.

It was observed that the self-help group composition initially fall in the line of kinship bonds and then immediately after internal discussion among the members they rearranged themselves on the line of caste and friendship. Some elements of distrust was marke among the kin members and thereafter they opted for multi-caste composition. However although it was not intended, among the self-help groups, the leadership remained with the upper caste females. All the members were drawn from the similar work culture and poorland less categories. Some had the skills and techniques of their family occupations such as weaving and pot making, brass making, stone engraving, wood craft, biri rolling and leather tanning in small scale, etc. The women through repeated interaction with the MASS personnel realised that in non-farm activities they can have a greater scope to change their socio-economic status provided they do not encounter barriers of severe type and they overcome the huddles. The total period of the micro credit operation through SSG in these two referred Blocks can be segmented into three phases : the initial phase, the awareness phase and the participatory phase. Each phase may be described for their salient features.

During the initial phase the women were apprehensive, and had to struggled to get permission from their male authoritarians. The village leaders were pathetic to the issue of SSG since it is purely women-based. There was low response and almost no interest shown by the male and female folks for the poor households due to the fact that they could never imagine that the poor also can go for saving for her future. Most of them were stubborn and failed to see beyond the influenced area of male world. The housewives were motivated to spare one fistful of rice every day and store in one common pitcher which was sold in the weekly market and the amount generated were becoming the self-raised funds. The amount generated were kept under the care of more than two members joint account. The objective was to take loan from it with marginal rate of interest and use them for income generating purposes and also to meet the exigencies. Thus a mini bank has been created to be controlled and governed by them to their own benefits. To facilitate it the NGO had added Rs.100 to their fund thus it was realised by the members that their social solidarity and group behaviour can provide them economic supports.

The second phase was identified by the rise of awareness of female-folk of wage earning families. The discussion groups formed in this phase who gathered courage to attend the periodic meeting organised by the NGO. There were debates and discussion on the modus operandi of the SSG. The experimental SSGs could act as a spring board to make members realised the social dynamics of the SSGs. The traditional moneylenders opposed the SSG moves and circulated imaginary stories that carries the defame contents for the female group formation. There were few family strives between the husband and wife centring the involvement of the housewives in SSGs for economic and political reasons. The meetings were assuming the feature of public platform to discuss on the female discrimination and harassments at home and in work sites by the employers. The mutual ventilation of problems encountered before the group not only yielded solutions but also strengthen the group dynamics so much so that the co-members ventured to meet the husband of the harassed in order to find out solution. This has exerted moral pressure on the male to become considerate. Many a times the meeting could not start due to intervention of village leaders and some time the members were not allowed to attend the meetings. There were wife beating increased in frequency and in two cases there was temporary separation in response to the growing women solidarity at village level. The village rich did not tolerate this and used their husbands against their move duping them through liquor. The encounters the women SSG members had to face was directly against their subordination at home and against the village rich to liberate their family from evil clutch. The women empowerment could be realised when they decided to fight against the liquor vendors and periodic meeting to find out solutions for some problems.

The third phase is marked its success. The participation of the members gradually increased in size and the issues of resources management came to fore. The members were found to participate among themselves and with the volunteers, raise questions to the government officials for their legitimate rights, imitate the new skill that would enhance their income generating capacity, felt acquiring some amount of freedom to decide for themselves and their children, emergence of female leadership and move ahead for negotiation with the husband at the home front and with the employer, and avoid handing over their income to the husband. The husbands came to the terms of compromise and no more ignored while dealing with the vital residential issues such as marriage of the children, giving land on contract for share cropping, and disposing off the stable property, etc. The women were found to enter into the hither to areas of male prerogative such as dealing with real estate adopting someone as their son/daughter, attending non-formal education centres, making husband to give them company to the Panchayat and Block Office for loan and subsidies, etc.

To purchase seeds, clothes, food, medicine and meet other exigencies the women could get financial support from the fund they have raised. They could dare to attend the meetings organised by the MASS for a period of two days at a walkable distance from their native villages and were found speaking the audience through loud-speaker with babies at their lap. To remain away for two days leaving the household works with the husband at home is really an achievement for them. The members feel proud of their SSGs for increasing the fund strength and membership and the transparency in financial dealings. The wife beating has drastically reduce and the sexual exploitation by the village rich has also declined. In fact to raise status the SSG has been used by the women as a spring board. The women learn about the basic book-keeping fodder and nursery development, panchayati raj system, use of natural manure and pest control mechanism, mode of participation in pani panchayat, community forest management and also about gender equality and human rights. That the male members of the small holders and the landless peasant households as valuable and scarce human resource are now put to task in right perspectives and made to realise that the women contribute no less than their counterparts.

There are many other mile stones too. They have acquired the skill of community fund management where women run their own lending and borrowing procedure to other women. Now the bank gives loan to SSGs through the NGOs with an intention that in due course of time they can run their own cooperative movement to build solidarity creating sense of we feeling among the members. The predictable resistance from the male folk that they had at the initial phase has now pushed back to their memory. There has been a remarkable difference from what they were and what they are today. The leaders said we were not having courage to meet the officials and could not ventilate our grievances with confidence now we go even to RDC and Collectors office and the police to ask for our rights. The inner strength that the women gathered through the SSGs (Small Saving Groups) and SHGs (Self Help Groups) has added new areas of their life style.

Referring to the western society Currie in his recent study on politics of hunger in Kalahandi had stated that despite the broadening of political and civil rights that has often accompanied modern citizenship, many people still lack the necessary resources such as food, clothing, shelter, physical security, access to information, education reasonable health and had also generalised stating that in many countries some groups remain incapable of excising their rights and obligations (2000; 223). The poor suffer but poor women are the more sufferers than the poor. To come out of the clutches of poverty the small but humble attempt for self help group and small saving as a strategy has been adopted by the women in rural sector. However, ail the women who came with strong conviction of self image and committed of the SSGs are not free from their dependence on male members. The wanted control of the members of SSG ha reduced indicating the change in their status. Status of women normally evaluated form the literacy level, demographic representation, nutritional status, representation in employment scenario, participation in decision making process, entry to the resources, other forms of relative discrimination and exploitation, enjoying citizenship rights and the rights own property, privilege and political power and other such rights. There are many angles of defining her status. Considering the above it has been felt that the status of women may be assessed as per the following formula:

$$S = \frac{TI-TE}{TW+TJ} X\ UI$$

Where S refer to Status, TI to total issues, TE refers to total encounters, TW refers to total issues went in favour of the women and TJ refers to total issues jointly settled by husband and wife. UI refers to undecided issues.

Status

$$= \frac{\text{Total number of major issues—Total number of encounters that went in favour of male members in family}}{\text{Total number of major issues went in women favour + Total number of issues jointly settled}} \times \text{Undecided issues}$$

The status of women with SSG membership was compared with women without SSG membership in the village. This was done among the small holders and the landless households. It was found that where the women have asserted their position and used the SSG as their support the result comes more than 1 and reverse is with more than -I. This implies that at grassroots the economic power derived through group action provides strength to women and enhances their status. And those who have less quantum of wanted control are found to be relatively better than others. The women with SSG intervention raise their awareness and become rich in knowledge through participation however in it the NGOs act as facilitators. It is observed that when women have the urge to organise themselves into coalitions and networks, exchange experiences and claim their economic, social and cultural rights at home front and outside with their group strength they are likely to change their status and emancipate them effectively which ultimately bring the social change minimising the discrimination and exploitation.

At the political frontiers her participation came quite late and her struggle for equal rights and opportunities across the countries remind the readers her sacrifice and her unwanted encounters. So long they remained invisible and do not raise voice to get their minimum rights there were social problems and initially things went serious. Irrespective of the developed and developing nations in the areas of political rights the women has been taken as less desired alternative. Till now gender biased occupations dominate the employment scenario. The historical texts have revealed that, in response to the struggle of women at various forums, some of the highly developed nations had to provide scope to their female citizens to take part in national politics. Like the class hierarchy, gender inequality has been the remarkable feature at the global scenario. Even if a few females occupy important position at the national and international level they depend very much on the male power. This confirms the one of the kinship principle suggested by Robin for where he stated that male exercises power over female.

The textual evidences from the earlier writings in India made by mostly male writers revealed that during prehistoric and proto-historic period the status of women was better. The women were regarded as at par with men and during Mahabharat and Puranic era however by and large they were projected as a symbol of sacrifice, compassion, and tolerance. Only during crisis when she remains no more capable of tolerating the exploitation and harassment her power could be gauged that manifested in form of destruction. Her status was a complementary to the status of male members in all rituals. During post-Vedic period and there after there was a steady decline in the power of women. During this phase of time the texts revealed that women were human beings of lesser human qualities.

The caste-class hierarchical syndrome in India and sex based occupations have kept women at the receiving ends been the dominant phenomena in contemporary societies. The female labour participation has been influenced by the caste factor however that is not the sole determining factor of female employment outside the home and village. The decline of caste based crafts due to industrialisation and mechanisation like weaving mat making pottery doll making, etc. has put the female out of employment. The middle and upper caste destitute female folks of village could participate by remaining at home in employment avenues such as husking, making puffed rice, silk worming, papad mad, pickle making, etc. With the invention of small technology and small scale industry they had to loose their earning sources. It has also been observed that any form of development has displaced female first from her skill, knowledge, power and rights.

With the rise of urbanisation and opening of new employment avenues women could also get sedentary jobs in formal as well as informal sectors and for this they had to encounter role conflicts. Women around the world hope for the future for better lives for themselves education and prosperity for their families. A broad array of social and economic changes is necessary to overcome the poverty, lack of education and limited control over their own lives that often keep women's hope coming true. But women can take an important step forward when they make their own reproductive choices about marriage, sex, child bearing and contraception.

Access to land, house right and movable and immovable properties will facilitate women's contribution on development. The power is gazed through the person's right to dispose off the stable property at her will and have planned investment of money for long-term productive purpose at their rational decisions. Relative economic stability and constant support of group cohesion and collective bargaining generates inner strength. Thus the confidence gained in the processes through the Small Saving Groups and Self-Help Groups the women of today can think of a better tomorrow.

BIBLIOGRAPHY

Currie, B., 2000 : *The Politics of Hunger in India : a Study of Democracy, Governance and Kalahandi's Poverty.* Chennai, Mac Million India Ltd.

Dube, L., 1975 : "Women's world- three encounters". In : *Encounters and Experiences.* A. Beteille and T.N. Madan (Eds.) New Delhi, Vikas Publishing House.

Ellen, R.F., 1984 : *Ethnographical Research : a Guide to General* Conduct.

Sydney, Academic Press.

Encyclopaedia Britannica, 2001 : Delux edition, CD Ram. Mead, M., 1977 : *Letters from the field - 1925:1975.* New York, Harer and Row.

Mohanti, P., 1995 : *My village, my India Nanpur : A Portrait of an Indian Village.* Corgi Books : a divison of Transworld Publishers Ltd., London.

Okely, J., 1983 : *The Travellers Gypsies.* Cambridge, Cambridge University Press.

Panda, P., H. Samantaraya and A.K. Mohanty, 1988-89 : Male P.G. students, their views on dowry and its implications-preliminary sociological analysis, *Jr. Manav,* 3 : 159-169.

APPENDIX

Case :

Gurubari a married illiterate aged around 35, one of the beneficaries belonging to weaver caste, of the SSG of a multi-village of Jujumara Block displayed samples of her coloured Sambalpuri sari prepared by her without taking any sort of help from her husband. She said that 'once my children go to school and husband go out for wage earning, I am free at home'. Taking loan from our group she had purchased thread and weaved the clothes. She sold two sets of clothes in the last weekly market and got a good amount. She saw a bag with the researcher and suddenly opined that she can prepare such bags and within a week it was found that she did it as a marketable item. With lot of proud she had shown the passbook starting with Rs 20 per member they now have almost 48 thousands in saving.

Kuntala, another middle aged woman has shown her small shop with consumable items worth of around 2000. She said that every day she gets a profit of about Rs.50 to Rs.60 sales. From the profit she could repair roof her house and made the floor cemented. Now she lead a good life. Both of them said that funds they got easily and they learnt book keeping and now dare to meet the local officials for development activities.

Others sitting under a tree discussing to purchase bamboo and make baskets cooperatively. One of them told "we can take loans from our own money at low rate of interest, we need not go to outsiders". This was being supported by other members. The village club house locally known as *dera ghar* is being used by the members to discuss their problems which includes the bad treatment of the husband, sickness of the family members, training inputs they got from NGO and take measures with the knowledge of other members. The perceptible change they stated was a reduction of family strives and migration to urban centres. The gossip groups often take the shape of discussion group on important village issues. With the intervention of MASS, the SSGs and SHGs assume the role of facilitating, motivating, training and information disseminating agency. The NGO had organised a meeting inviting around 68 SSGs to distribute boxes to the village self help groups. Almost all the members came. It was observed that the members who never went out of the village could talk their success to the large audience through mike-set fearlessly and with confidence.

Their cooperative movement has built solidarity and created a sense of belonging and bonding. The resistance posed by male folk against during their initial stage now no more oppose them attending the meetings. From the silence form of protest at home against the male members who did not bother their desire, they have reached a stage of making their male members to listen and support them in their endeavour. Many members are seen self-confident and their inner strength that the SSGs built has placed these women in good stead for the forthcoming days. Women have done for themselves and their families they have joined hands, fought and got and can go ahead a long way to get their due, they said.

3

Dalit Women, Dalit Literature and Anthropology

N.K. Das

The Dalits have faced centuries of oppression. For centuries they had lived at the mercy of their rich high caste masters. Under the impact of new thoughts, democratic political institutions and economy, the old structural and functional bases of the villages are crumbling. There is a new awakening among the Dalits today, their strivings to gain human dignity. The Scheduled Castes, Scheduled Tribes and other backward classes in many parts of India have increasingly identified themselves as 'Dalit' (the oppressed). This emerging pan - Indian identity has been widely recognised in recent years. Anthropologists and Sociologists are however not in agreement unanimously about pragmatic relevance of this term. Historian Romila Thapar maintains that there is a political necessity for holding on the Dalit category. She traces the roots of this category in Pali literature in which Dalit means "the oppressed". Some scholars have argued that any attempt to accord a pan-Indian status to this category would rob other identities based on region and culture (Pandian and others, quoted in *Guru and Geetha* 2000). Gajendran has noted that upper caste common sense saw Dalits as uncultured and primitive people doing menial jobs and lacking a written antiquity (*Guru an Geetha* 2000). Pleading extension of the Dalit category, Illiah has advocated for inclusion of the category Bahujan within the Dalit category. Rege urges that the Dalit Feminism should be treated differently from the standpoint of epistemology (*Guru and Geetha* 2000).

I

The Scheduled Castes, Scheduled Tribes and the other backward classes together constitute about 60 per cent of India's population. They together form the Dalit category. There are as many as 600 communities which are regarded as Scheduled Castes. The Scheduled Castes alone constitute 15.75 per cent of the country's population (Khillare 1997). The genesis of Dalit category is associated with social movements among the scheduled castes in Maharashtra, where the Scheduled Castes identified themselves as Dèlit. In this chapter also we will concentrate on the Scheduled Castes in different parts of India. The people of India project of the Anthropological Survey of India has identified 450 Scheduled Castes, including 45 unlisted sub-groups. The total number of Scheduled Caste segments come to 751 (Singh, 1995). Numerically speaking, the Chamar outrank all other castes. Other numerically large Scheduled Castes, widely distributed in different parts of India, are Adi Dravida, Pasi, Madiga, Dusadh, Mala, Pariyan, Dhobi, Adi-Karnataka and Mahar. The Harijans, the 'Untouchables', were earlier identified as 'Depressed classes'. From 1935 onwards they came to be known as Scheduled Castes. Besides agricultural labour, the Scheduled Castes had traditionally worked as scavengers, grave-diggers, dead-cattle removers, tanners and shoe-makers.

Both the Scheduled Castes and Scheduled Tribes constitute the Dalit social category, but there are certain aspects in which the problems of the Scheduled Castes and Scheduled Tribes differ. The Scheduled Tribes mainly suffer from geographical isolation and being forest dwellers, their society is generally characterised by low level of techno-economic development. The Scheduled Castes, on the other hand suffer not only from economic backwardness, they also suffer from social disabilities and stigma. The lowness of the Scheduled Caste is ritually explained by their *permanent impurity* which derives from their association with death and organic pollution. They fulfil certain essential ritual function within Indian society. "They remove impurity from the social world" (Deliege 1992). Untouchability stands abolished by virtue of Article 17 of the Constitution and its practice in any form is punishable, but social discriminations against the Scheduled Castes still linger in many parts of the country. Thus, 76, 748 cases of atrocities against persons belonging to Scheduled Castes and 17,101 cases of atrocities against Scheduled Tribes were reported between 1986-1990. Of these, 5339 cases were of rape.

Historically speaking, these so-called ritually low caste groups had constituted the artisan and service class and provided services to high castes and rich landowners, under a rigid *jajmani* system in the past. Of the total Scheduled Castes population 88 per cent lives in villages. Broadly speaking, north India has greater concentration of Scheduled Caste communities than south India. In post-independence era, allotment of agricultural land to landless Scheduled Castes families under land reforms or as a consequence of reclamation of agricultural land has strengthened their proportion in the primary sector as owner - cultivator. But these measures have hardly led to the diversification of occupational structure of the Scheduled Castes population to any great extent. Agricultural labour thus continues to be the main occupation of the Scheduled Castes. It is followed by cultivation, other services, manufacturing industries, livestock, plantations, fishing, storage, transport and communication, trade and commerce, construction, mining and quarrying in this order (Chandana 1989 : 151).

The link between technology, female participation in agricultural production and the social status of women was first proposed at global level by Boserup. It has been argued that in rural areas the type of agricultural system determines not only female participation but also the sex ratio and the system of control over, an inheritance of, property. In this respect in north and south of India we may notice some contrasts. In south India because of greater rice cultivation, unlike wheat cultivation in north India, women are regarded as more valuable.

Perusal of census and other reports, in the context of comparison of the geography of female participation with complex agricultural regions shows certain congruence between "Wheat region (Punjab,

Haryana) and low female participation rates" on the one hand and the "Rice region (Tamil Nadu, Andhra Pradesh) and high female participation" on the other. High female participation rates are also be found, however, in semi-arid tropical areas while low female participation is observed in stock rearing in Rajasthan, or with diversified agriculture in UP. The participation of women is not only a function of the gender division of labour, but also a need of poverty. Since a greater proportion of population is landless in southern Indian rice areas than in northern wheat belt, female participation will be higher in south (Harris and Watson 1987). But landlessness is not a sole factor. In Haryana, women are drawn into the agricultural wage labour force not only from the ranks of the landless but also from small farming households. Besides poverty, caste, kinship and marriage indeed are the chief institutional and social factors influencing female participation in wage labour. In the north, where female as a rule do not inherit property, they are accompanied with dowry, and bride necessarily moves from natal - locality. In the south, women may and sometimes do inherit property (Harris and Watson 1987). Local cross-cousin marriage within the caste is the norm, and land tends to be retained within a close group of kindred, and on occasions bride price may be transferred. Its purpose is to recompense the bride givers for the loss of a potential earner ('selling' the bride) or is to be used to gain wives for her brothers (Harris and Watson 1967).

The circumstances and factors, which influence the extent of female participation in agricultural and allied activities, vary widely across different regions of India. Within each region female participation in labour work is influenced by -

(a) Agro - climatic base and crop cultural practice,

(b) Distribution of assets (land) among rural households,

(c) Presence of the Scheduled Castes and Scheduled Tribes, and

(d) The skill and educational background of female population (Jose 1989 :15).

Increased entry of women into the lowest rungs of the skill hierarchy as agricultural labourers and unskilled workers has only contributed to aggravate the process of women's marginalisation. Consequently, they tend to be relegated into subordinate and inferior positions in terms of wage levels, employment status and nature and intensity of work in relation to male workers. Opportunities for upward occupational mobility are indeed virtually non-existent for women workers.

The female literacy among the Scheduled Castes has always been extremely low, more so in rural areas. Only one female out of every thirty-three females in rural areas could be classified as literate among the Scheduled Castes. There are however some exceptions in some parts of India. Further, the Scheduled Castes like Dhenuwar, Karnakan or Padanna and Pathiyan had more than two-thirds of their population as literate (Chandana 1989 : 149). Gender disparities in return to the sale of labour reflects gender disparities in return to the human capital embodied in labour, that is, for any given level of human capital, women received lower returns (Lipton, 1993).

Rajuladevi examines the poverty profiles of landless female labour households in wet and dry villages of Tamil Nadu. Using Marxist class analysis, Rajuladevi (2000) observed that landless women and their husbands experienced poverty differently and often unequally. In the labour market, the women are 'inferior bearers of labour'. Hence the women are paid low wages. Rajuladevi (2000) further observed that 'Landless women labourers in both wet and dry villages had borrowed large amount to meet their day to day consumption needs'. Gender based 'contractual inferiority'. (White Head 1985) in rural India derives from women's greater material dependence within the household, higher rates of illiteracy, poor clothing, fewer collateral generating assets, coupled with their general in-experience in the domain of public institutions. During the slack season when there is no work and no wages, women are driven to borrow. In a patriarchal society she gets no credit : she must obtain the signature and collateral of husbands/fathers/son.

Despite presence of rice belts in southern and eastern region, true peasants - owner - cultivators - are insignificant in number (Das, Veena 1976). Cheap labour is abundantly available in this region (Sinha 1993). In most parts of eastern India and parts of MP (and Chhattisgarh) both men women from lower strata (so-called Dalits) work in the fields together. In a tribal society in MP, where both men and women work in fields the major decision-making powers rest in men, for they argue that "The income of the man is necessary for staple crops, the income of the women only contributes towards the cost of salt (Das, Veena 1976).

The above review reveals that there are both regional and caste variations in terms of marginalisation of women in respective societies. Difference in property relations, land management, crop-produce pattern in varied ecological zones, landlessness, social stratification and patriarchal cultural values have indeed differently placed constraints on freedom and autonomy of Dalit women, but there is little evidence to suggest that women have access to more power and authority in the south than in north or eastern India. The rural Dalit women everywhere have been equally denied social freedom and are subjected to identical oppressive practices.

We observed that linkages between gender, caste and class, structure the organisation of production, reproduction and redistribution. Two most important orientations which have been brought to centre of Dalit feminist standpoint are 'caste' and 'contemporary capitalism' (Rege 2000; Datar 1999). Caste in mediating the control over resources and the division of labour structures the divide between intellectual and manual labour. The inter-linkages between caste based division of labour and sexual division of labour control the production of life through the marriage circles and make way for patriarchal extraction of women's subsistence agricultural as a sign of strength (Rege 2000). We need not view environmental degradation as merely a result of industrial growth and technology or faulty state policies but have to locate the degradation as an integral part of the existence growth and constitution of contemporary capitalism (Bapat 1996 quoted in Rege 2000; Agarwal 1992).

Dalit women in some parts of India in recent years have mobilised themselves to fight for their rights on natural resources. In fact, the decade of the 1970s was marked by a series of forest movements, involving women folk in different parts of the country. Ecologists and environmentalists have been aggressively involved in campaigning in rural, coastal, forest and hill areas focusing on the rights of the rural Dalit people. According to Medha Patekar 'The mass movements with the environmental vision have a great role to play (Patekar 2000).

Driven by hunger and starvation, Dalit women in many parts of India, have come forward and taken lead in forming local-level committees to fight for their rights on local natural resources, illegally captured by forward castes. Several such success stories have been reported in Bihar. They are worth mentioning.

It is the forward caste landlords and moneylenders who capture the thousands of ponds, rivulets and water logged areas in north Bihar and exploit the resources to their advantage. In these areas, as reported by Mukul Sharma (2000) the Dalits such as Mallahs, a fisherfolk caste, the Musahars, the lowest among the Scheduled Castes and other low castes, have been fighting to claim their legitimate rights. Fishing rights in these ponds are legally those of the Dalits living near these water bodies. In 1999 some Dalits took control of some ponds near their villages. An NGO, Lok Shakti Sangatham, since 1992 is working in this area for Dalit causes. In this region the leases for fishing are given by Government to Fishermen Co-operative societies, to be allotted fully for the benefit of the Mallahs. But they face problems. The ponds are controlled by rich landowners, even when they are officially leased out to the Mallahs or Mushahar. A common mode adopted is to take the lease in the name of Mallah or Mushahar who is heavily indebted to a landowner/moneylender. It is latter who controls everything and sells the produce. With the help of Lok Shakti Sangathan the Dalits are protesting for their rights. While fighting for one Tiwari pond in village Soharai Brahamotar, in

1993, the Dalit women took initiative and hold a meeting. Tense situation prevailed for over an year. The landowner and his men threatened the villagers. Slowly the villagers came out of their fear and in 1994 they decided to approach the administration. In 1996-97, they digged the pond. Ultimately they won. Now the Dalit control the ponds through their committees. Sirpur Musahari is a village of the Dalit Musahars, in Madhubani district. When the Dalits formed a Sangathan in early 1990s, the first thing they did was to claim their rights over ponds. The Dalit women occupied the pond by force. Since 1995 the Dalit have the right over the pond. They guard it day and night. In yet another instance, credit goes to the Dalit women of Haithiwadi village of Madhubani district for forming a society of their own since 1994 and for liberating as many as 31 ponds around their village (Sharma 2000). These success stories of the illiterate Dalit women of North Bihar may be seen as true instances of Eco-feministic movement in rural India.

II

Literary expression goes hand in hand with political agitation. The Dalits have variously expressed resentment and dissent in different parts of India in different historical phases. Dalit literature, which has been identified as a liberation literature is part of Dalit culture. The Dalits indeed have their own unique vocabulary and speech. Dalit literature is people's literature and at the same time the feminist literature. Shame, sexual exploitation, anger, sorrow and persistent hope are the main content of Dalit literature. Dalit literature has a long tradition in south India (Karnataka, Tamil Nadu and Andhra Pradesh). Thus, a Dalit woman, Kalavve, challenged the upper castes in the twelfth century in the following words :

Those who eat goats, fowl and tiny fish,
Such, they call caste people.
Those, who eat the sacred cow,
that showers frothing milk for Shiva,
Such, they call 'out-castes'.

In the same poem, Kalavve points out how Brahmans drink with glee water and ghee from bags made of cattle hide by untouchable (Shiva Prakash 1999). Dharman (1999) argues that the problem of the Dalits has not sprung up in recent years. Dalit issues and the 'Voices' pleading the Dalit causes have been raised from the very beginning of Tamil literature. In one such old writing the Siddas had questioned :

* Is the pleasure of upper class women's flesh different from that of Pariah woman's? Do the flesh, bone and skin of women bear the stamp of their caste?

Now we have a sizeable body of Dalit literature not only in Tamil and Kannada, but also in Telugu, Marathi, Hindi, Gujarati, Punjabi and Bengali. In Andhra Pradesh we have not only a rich tradition of Dalit literature mainly contributed by Gaddar, but non-Dalit sections of exploited people, such as the Madiga, have come out with challenging voices.

Gaddar, the popular, Telugu singer - poet, embodies many institutions in his struggle to re-shape the structure of caste/class system. As a Dalit he wrote hundreds of songs that brought the Dalit Bahujan working class and women's life into literary texts. An early song (Ilaiah 1997) that won the hearts of Telugu society was written around the life experience of his mother :

Oh, mother,
Lachumamma,
your blouse is torn,
your hair is soiled,
your sari is torn,
you have no money to buy new ones.
Even in that condition
what have you done?
You planted saplings
walking backwards like a bull
in order to produce
food from the mud.

It was no accident that Gorky's most popular novel is about the mother's role in revolution. Gaddar's most popular song is also about a Dalit mother's role in the production of wealth (Illaiah 1997). Gaddar used a powerful song by another Dalit poet, Guda Anjaiah to educate the poor. When Gaddar sang Ea Vuru Manadira (this village is ours), thousands of people joined him in procession.

Gaddar constructs the producing castes and classes as *matti chetulu* (the hands that turn mud into food). He uses the basic Dalit - Bahujan language, idiom and symbolism by transforming the linguistic structure of literary Telugu. Gradually his influence spread to cinema. Gaddar's association with the Ambedkarite movement and thought raised new hopes.

In all his songs about women, the institution of the family comes under attack :

Mogolla nollallo beedilai Kaletollam,
nindu amasanaadu 'o' Lachgummadi,
Aada pilla puttinaadi 'o' Lachagummadi
'We women, burn as cigars in the mouths of men,
if a girl is born on a no-moon day, the
mother is forced to throw her away (Illaiah 1997).
About Dalit life, Gaddar sings :
'matti batukulu -
yetti batukulu.

'Dalit lives are not only the lives that live in soil, but they are bonded lives' as well (Illaiah 1997).

Shame, anger, sorrow and indomitable hope have always been main content of Dalit literature of the past present[2]. The relationship between such radical traditions of the past and present day Dalit literary movements, particularly those concerned with women's issues, need to be reviewed and analysed anthropologically in order not only to project the insider's perspective but also to 'deconstruct' pre-conceived notions and presumptions of the past.

III

Women remained till recently invisible in anthropology. Though they appeared in the literature in the context of 'kinship and marriage' but 'analysis of social reality were loaded with a distinct male bias which led to the distortion of facts, (Moore 1988). In most of Indian anthropological works of earlier period traditional familial roles of women were glorified (Mehrotra 1990) which was only to justify the patriarchal domination of men-folk. Veena Majumdar (1986) has identified three ingredients in an Indian perspective on women's studies: (1) Acceptance and recognition of Indian society as plural society, (2) Recognition that women must fight for future and her involvement in political, economic and social processes in all levels and (3) That research and policy have to be pro-women. Leela Dube (1980) stated that women's studies have been handicapped by a general lack of understanding of cross-cultural and inter cultural variations in the organisational principles of societies and in the life contexts of women (1980).

A new emphasis on women as a person, as gender category is emerging as a recent trend in anthropology. Symbolic anthropologists are focusing on woman's body, her sexuality, notion of femininity and different metaphors used in language and culture to represent reality (Veena Das 1988; Dube; 1986, 1988). Using cross- cultural data Sandy (1973) examined the theory[3] of status of women on the basis of ecological and economic factors and concluded that female production is a necessary but not sufficient for the development of female power and that female status is likely to develop if women have control over valued products and strategic resources (Sandy, 1973). Khare (1998) has argued that 'World anthropology today is multi-centred. In India, the problems of the socially disadvantaged categories of people may not be ignored any longer. The anthropologist should not only be a seeker of truth but also of social justice. With specific reference to Dalit women and other powerless categories of people, Khare, says 'Anthropology is writing about culture or, more perceptively, "Writing culture", and unless this is done with (not about) the people, unless it incorporates and not merely appropriates their voices, 'doing' anthropology will be in vain'. Khare quotes Dalit woman, "When others write about us, they misrepresent us, otherwise, we are mostly ignored or overlooked. This body is over of life" (Khare 1998 : 161f). There is no doubt that there has emerged a keen self awareness and a sense of having been wronged and abused, on part of the oppressed.

Notes

1. The views expressed in this paper are those of author only.

2. In their book *Viramma : Life of a Dalit,* J. Racine and J.L. Racine (2000) provide an 'Autobiography of a Dalit woman (transcribed into English). In her autobiography, Viramma, the Dalit woman, says, "Her illiteracy, her ignorance of genuine connections between events, her lack of information, her lack of access to modern communication have stood in the way of her improving her social position". She further says, "The hierarchy of the castes was actually a graded access to land and a graduated share of the harvest." She also says ".... Political parties and political power are meant only to be manipulated in order to move up...." (Racine and Racine 2000).

3. The Human Development Report 1995 demonstrates that no country in the world treats women as well as it does its men. The term social status seems to be more of an artificial construct. It is generally agreed that, instead of use of term status we should be concerned with the placement of women in a system of access to power, property and legal and economic freedom. Term status is considered to be more limited in scope. Hence the term women's autonomy has gained currency in development and feminist literature. The women's autonomy denotes the independence the women have in their functioning.

References

Agrawal, Bina, 1992: 'The Gender and Environment Debate : Lessons from India', *Feminist Studies,* Vol. 18, No.1.

Bapat, Ram, 1996: *Arthakarnachya Badalatya Disha.* Satara : Ambedkar Academy.

Chandana, R.C., 1989: *Spatial dimensions of scheduled castes in India.* New Delhi : Intellectual Publishing House.

Das, Veena, 1976: 'Indian Women : Work, Power and Status', in *Indian Women* at Ed. B.R. Nanda. New Delhi : Vikas Publication.

Das, Veena, 1988: 'Femininity and the Orientation to the body' in *Education, Socialisation and Women.* Ed. Karuna Chanana. New Delhi : Orient Longman.

Datar, Chhaya, 1999: Non-Brahmin Renderings of Feminism in Maharashtra, *Economic and Political Weekly,* October 9, 1999.

Deliege, Robert, 1992: Replication and Consensus, Untouchability, Caste and Ideology in India, *Man.,* 27, 1 : 155-73.

Dharman, Cho, 1999: 'What is said and what ought to have been said' *Indian Literature.* 193 : 91-93.

Dube, Leela, 1980. *Review of studies on women in South East Asia.* UNESCO.

Dube, Leela, 1986: Seed and Earth : 'The symbolism of biological reproduction and sexual relations of production'. In *Visibility and Power.* Eds. L. Dube, E. Leacock and S. Ardener. pp. 22-53. Delhi : Oxford University Press.

Dube, Leela, 1988: 'On the construction of Gender : Hindu girls in Patrilineal India' in *Education, Socialisation and Women.* Ed. K. Chanana. New Delhi : Orient Longman.

Guru, Gopal and V. Geetha, 2000: New phase of Dalit-Bahujan intellectual activity. *Economic and Political Weekly,* January 15, 2000.

Harriss, B. and E. Watson, 1987: The sex ratio in South Asia in *Geography of Gender in the Third World.* Eds. J.H. Momsen and J. Townsend, London : Hutchinson.

Ilaiah, Kancha, 1997: Gaddar : Embodying many institutions. *Seminar,* 456 August, 1997.

Jose, A.V., 1989: 'Female labour force participation in India' in *Limited Options* Ed. A.V. Jose. New Delhi : I.L.O. Publications.

Khare, R.S., 1998: *Cultural Diversity and Social Discontent.* New Delhi : Sage.

Khillare, Y., 1997: *Present Status of Backward Classes in India.* Aurangabad : Centre for studies on SC. ST.

Lipton, Michael, 1983: *Labour and Poverty.* Working Paper 16. Washington DC World Bank.

Majumdar, V., 1986. 'Indian perspectives to women's studies' in *Women's Studies in India,* Ed. M. Krishnaraj, New Delhi (London) : Sargam Books.

Mehrotra, Nilika, 1990: 'Women's issues in Indian Anthropology'. *The Eastern Anthropologist.* Vol. 43, No. 2.

Moore, H.L., 1988: *Feminism and Anthropology.* London : Polity Press.

Patekar, Medha, 2000: 'People's movements' *Survey of the Environment. The Hindu.* Chennai.

Racine, J. and J.C. Racine, 2000: *Life of a Dalit by Viramma.* Delhi: Social Science Press.

Rajuladevi, A.K., 2000: Profiles in poverty. *Economic and Political Weekly,* February 5, 2000.

Rege, Sharmila, 2000: 'Real Feminism and Dalit Women' *Economic and Political Weekly,* February 5, 2000.

Sandy, P.S., 1973: Towards a theory of the status of Women. *American Anthropologist.* 75 : 5

Sharma, Mukul, 2000: 'Dalit Rights'. *Survey of the Environment. The Hindu.* Chennai.

Shiva Prakash, H.S. 1999: 'The out-caste at the city gate' *Indian Literature.* 193 : 5-11.

Sinha, S.C., 1993: *Anthropology of weaker sections,* New Delhi : Concept Publication.

Singh, K.S. 1995: *The Scheduled Castes* (Second Edition). Calcutta: Anthropological Survey of India.

Whitehead, A., 1985: 'Effects of Technological Change on Rural Women' in *Technology and Rural Women.* I. Ahmed (Ed.) London : G.A. and Unwin.

4
Status of Indian Women in Thailand*

Surendra K. Gupta

Indians started migrating to South-East Asia sometime in the second or third century B.C.Traders and merchants were attracted by fabulous quantities of gold and other precious minerals besides the spices found there. These traders and merchants came from all parts of India and belonged to different castes among Hindus and other religious groups. Since it was difficult to cross High Mountain terrain, sea route was frequently used for travelling. The knowledge and experience gained by these people induced other traders and also encouraged other people from different walks of life to migrate to South-East Asia. The credit for leaving the imprint of Indian culture and religion goes to King Asoka of Muryan empire (330 B.C. to 180 B.C.) who promoted Buddhism in several countries of South-East Asia. The trade relations between India and South-East Asia got boost from the first century A.D. onwards when some Indian migrants founded their own kingdom. The Indian influence in South-East Asia lasted for 1300 years and ended with the emergence of Thais as one of the major powers. Indianthe remnants of Indian culture can still be seen in Thai society. The Indian who

* This paper is apart of full length study conducted among Indians in Thailand by the author.

migrated to this region during this period assimilated themselves with the local people by marrying their women folk. These people were able to influence the culture of the local people but in the process lost their own identity. The best example of such peoples are Oriya Brahmans who live in a Hindu temple in Bangkok, known as Thai Brahmins. They have married local Thai women, speak only Thai language, eat Thai food and also represent Brahmins at all the royal ceremonies.

The present day Indians living in Thailand started migrating in 19th century when the British were granted permission to trade at Thailand's part in 1826. Since Indians who were British subjects at that time took the advantage and started settling in Thailand. The signing of the Bowring Treaty in 1855 and fourteen more treaties in the next fifteen years with other trading nations of Europe converted the self sufficient economy of Thailand into a dual economy ".. one part traditional and the other increasingly commercialized. The latter produced agricultural raw material and minerals for world market receiving in exchange manufactured goods" (Grilling, 1981; 45). Under the Bowring Treaty, the foreigners were granted extra territoriality and the British subjects were given the right to trade freely in all seaports and to reside permanently in Bangkok. This encouraged the British subjects like the Burmese and the Indians to migrate to Thailand. The declaration that Indians in any part of the British Empire had equal rights to those of any other of Her Majesty's subjects (Queen of England) helped them establish trading and commercial centres in Thailand.

The abolition of slavery in 1905 in Thailand resulted in an acute shortage of labour supply. Before its abolition the control of labour had been more crucial as the power of king, princes and nobles depended on the number of labourers under one's control. However, the growth of agriculture and the pressure of population on land made ownership of land more important. The permission to hire immigrant labour accorded by King Mongkut helped to solve the problem of labour shortage, especially after the abolition of slavery. Since the local Thais were not ready to work as hired labourers in plantation (rubber and teak) and in mining activities, Indian and Chinese immigrants filled the gap. The native people preferred to work in rice cultivation rather than on plantations.

Punjabis started migrating to Thailand in 1884 AD and it is said that in the beginning there were about 20 families of Punjabis and all of them lived in the Phaurat area only. Kirparam Madan who was a Sehajdhari Sikh came to Thailand in 1884 AD from Bhadewal village in Sliakot district (now in Pakistan) during the reign of King Chulalongkorn. Kirparam was a businessman and had travelled far and wide. During one of his visit of Thailand, when he was granted royal audience by the then king, Kirparam presented a beautiful horse to the king and the king reciprocated by giving him an elephant and other valuables. Kirparam gifted that elephant to the Maharaja of Jammu on behalf of the king of Thailand.

Kirparam's wife belonged to the Narula Sikh family of village Philloke in Gujaranwala district (now in Pakistan). She had five brothers. After his first visit to Bangkok, Kirparam decided to start a textile business in Bangkok. Later on his wife's brother joined him in his business and they worked together for three years. After three years, brother of Kirparam's wife started his own business and also called his younger brother to help him. In1890, these two brothers started their own firm called Messrs. L.S. Bhagwan Singh and company in the name of their father. Gradually, they were joined by others brothers and their families, and soon became one of the richest firms in Thailand. All the descendants of these brothers at present are running successful business in Bangkok. Kirparam who had his own business in Thailand also brought his eldest son first, and his second son followed him later. The grandsons of Kirparam are now doing their own business in Bangkok.

The third Punjabi family to migrate to Thailand was the family of the brother of the father of Kirparam's wife. Gradually other Sikhs and Hindus of the village Philoke started migrating to Thailand and by 1910 a large number of Punjabi's had settled in Thailand.

In the beginning the Punjabi's of three districts of the then Western Punjab namely Gujaranwala, Sekhopura and Sialkot migrated to Thailand. All of them belonged to the Arora caste and three sub-castes namely Madan, Narula and Chawla. Madan were the first to come, followed by Narula and Chawla. It was pointed out by many respondents that all the Punjabi migrants of the first wave were related to each other. At that time there was no distinction between a Hindu and a Sikh. It was a common practice for a family in Punjab to offer one of the sons to Sikhism. Thus, members of a family could belong to both the faiths. For instance, the first Punjabi migrant Kirparam was Hindu but his wife was from a Sikh family.

Gorakhpuri's also started migrating to Thailand around the late 19th century. It is said that some Gorakhpuris went to Burma after the first war of Indian Independence in 1857 due to fear of prosecution by the British for their role in the revolt. Since Burma was a part of India at that time, therefore, the Indians migrated to Thailand. In the beginning there were about 20 families of Gorakhpuris and all of them were dairymen. Since Thailand was considered as safe place, they decided to settle here and gradually brought their families and other relatives.

Quite a large number of Punjabi's and Gorakhpuris migrated to Thailand during the Second World War. There were many army personnel who were fighting for the British in Malaysia and Singapore and were disgusted by the discriminatory behaviour of the British officers in matters of promotion and other facilities, deserted the British army and joined hands with Indian revolutionaries to form the Indian Independence League with its main Centre in Bangkok. The Indian Independence League was later redesignated as the Indian National Army.

Gorakhpuris have also migrated to Thailand in large numbers from 1960 onwards. Most of them migrated with the sole purpose of making money and they did not mind doing any kind of work. Since immigration to Thailand has become very difficult the minority of these migrants come on a three months visa and after the expiry of their time they just cross over to Malaysia and reenter Thailand with a fresh visa for three months. In the beginning these people sell various items as vendors and once they pick up the language, they start the NGOEN-SOD business which is commonly called as Ding-Dong. In this they supply various items to locals who cannot afford these items. The people engaged in this business charge more from the locals but these people don't mind this as they are repaying in instalment.

History and pattern of migration of Punjabis and Gorakhpuris shows some distinct pattern of migration among them. Punjabi migration can be called as chain migration as one member has been followed by others and gradually the entire family and/or kin group, migrated to Thailand, leaving behind some distant relatives. Among Gorakhpuris very few families followed chain migration. The common pattern of migration among Gorakhpuris is relay migration. In relay migration only one member migrated at a time and when he went back he was replaced by another member. Punjabi mainly migrated to Thailand with the intention of settling down there where as among Gorakhpuris very few people migrated to settle.

Status of Punhabi Women

There was time when Sikhs were sending their girls to settle in India after marriage. Now, the girls, born and brought up in Thailand do not want to get married in India for fear of migrating back to India and getting adjusted in strange ervirons. Since Sikhs do not generally want their daughters to marry a Non-Sikh, they look for a suitable match in Thailand, failing that they look to neighbouring countries such as Hongkong, Malaysia and

Singapore. The other alternate is to "smuggle in " a suitable boy for their daughter who are gradually regularized as immigrants after the marriage.

Sikh women in Thailand have retained their traditional dress of *Salwar* (lose trousers) and *Kameez* (tunic covering the upper part of women's body) or *Sari*, but the young girls have start wearing Jeans and other western style dresses such as skirt, etc. All Sikh women, young and old, wear *Kara* (steel wrist-band) on their right wrist. At home the status of Sikh women has changed but not so noticeably. Now, wives and daughters have started sitting at family run shops and businesses, but they mostly help their menfolk. Some young girls have also started working as sales girls, secretaries and teachers.

Within the home the traditional relationships are maintained. Respect for one's elders are prized virtues even in a foreign land and all children are taught this. Most of the time children submit to their parents wishes in matters of education, vocation and marriage. Household chores continue to be the domain of women. A Punjabi house in Bangkok is a replica of typical Indian home. The difference between a prosperous and an ordinary house may be between the type of house, the quality of furniture and the quality of household goods.

Sikh women also visit Gurudwara regularly and celebrate all the religious festivals like Baisakshi and the birthdays of Sikh Gurus. All these functions are held in Gurudwara and Sikh women also attend these functions in large numbers.

The majority of Hindu Punjabi women wear their traditional dress of *Sari* and *Salwar Kameez,* though some women young and middle-aged have started wearing Jeans. They put bangles on their arms, the more prosperous wear gold bangles but a large majority of them wear glass bangles and also apply *bindi* on their forehead. A few Punjabi women sprinkle vermilion on their hair parting, a symbol of married women.

Like Sikh women, the status of Hindu women has also

changed though household chores continue to be their main activity. Some young girls and middle aged women have started participating in social, cultural and economic activities. A few Punjabi women have started helping their menfolk in business activities.

In most of the houses, one can find pictures of Hindu gods and goddesses like Ram, Krishna, Vishnu, Lakshmi and Durga. Hindu women are also seen to reserve one corner of their home for worship. The prosperous families keep a separate room for such purposes.

All Hindu Punjabi women speak Punjabi at home, but use Thai when they talk to local people. The younger generation females like to watch Thai and English movies, but also enjoy Indian music and films.

Some changes have been noticed in the marriage pattern of Hindu Punjabis. Earlier, the parents used to find suitable matches for their daughter from India, but now, the girls resist going to India after marriage. While selection a spouse for their wards, the preference is given to person of same caste and religion.

Punjabi ladies participate in all the functions held in Dev Samaj Mandir. On every Tuesday ladies *Satsang* is held in the temple premises. In the *Satsang* they sing Bhajans and Kirtan. The occasion is also used to celebrate the marriages and birth-days of their sons, daughters as well as that of grand children. The Hindu Punjabi ladies are very religious and celebrate fast and perform all Pujas.

Status of Gorakhpuri Women

Though Gorakhpuris also started migrating to Thailand almost at the same time as Sikhs and Hindu Punjabis, but they do not regard Thailand as their home. Those who migrated in the beginning had been replaced by their brothers and/or sons. Among Gorakhpuris, the relay migration had been and still is the dominant pattern.

A large number of Gorakhpuris have not brought their famlies and are living alone. This was and still is the prominent feature of Gorakhpuris. Some of them bring their families for brief visits. These people also visit India to meet their kinsfolk.

Living in Thailand has not affected the life style and dressing pattern of Gorakhpuris. Like males, the females also wear their traditional dresses like *Sarees*. They also wear glass bangles and apply a *bindi* on their forehead and sprinkle vermilion on their hair parting, a mark of their marital bliss. Gorakhpuri women do not go out for work. Almost all of them remain confined to home. Many of these women cover their heads (half veiling their faces) when they walk with their spouses in the city. Within the home, the Gorakhpuris are more traditional as compared to Sikhs and Hindu Punjabi. The girls submit to their parents wishes in terms of education and marriage. They send their wards especially the girls to India for education, as they do not want their daughters to expose to an alien culture. Gorakhpuri females never go out alone in the market and they are always accompanied by their male members even for a visit to the temple.

Visit to a Gorakhpuri family show no impact of living in a foreign country. Females do all the household work from cleaning to cooking. They prefer to eat their food in a stainless steel *Thali* (big plate) and eat Indian dishes only. Gorakhpuri females are very religious and observe and celebrate all the Indian religious festivals and also perform Puja regularly. They also visit temples frequently, no change has been noticed in the marriage pattern of Gorakhpuris. They send their daughters to India for marriage and also look for a suitable match from the same caste. They also match the horoscope of the boy and the girls before settling the marriage.

Conclusion

The differences in the status of Punjabi women (both Sikh as well as Hindu) and Gorakhpuri women can be attributed to differences in cultural, contextual and situational factors. Hindu Punjabi and Sikhs hail from the same region in Punjab and the cultural background of both these communities in more or less the same. Their level of acculturation in Thailand is also similar. They have created more apertures and are more open to new influences. A distinctive feature of Punjabi culture is their adaptability and openness to change. This is due to the fact that most alien cultures came to India from the north-west and Punjab being geographically closest to the border had the maximum impact. Thus Punjab became a melting post of various composite cultures, indigenous and foreign, which gradually were incorporated in what came to be known as Punjabi culture. This exposure helped Punjabis to have culture with a liberal outlook. Immigrants with this kind of background would certainly be more open and adaptable in a different society. Since both Hindu Punjabi and Sikhs migrated to Thailand with their families and with the intention of settling down their permanently they gave more freedom and liberty to their womenfolk. As a result the Punjabi women in Thailand are participating in economic activities and also take interest in other cultural, social and religious activities.

As compared to Hindu Punjabi and Sikhs, Gorakhpuris are more rigid and traditional. They hail from a region in India which is insulated and has not been exposed to other cultures. In Thailand they have isolated themselves and 'shy away' not only from local Thai's but also from other Indian groups also. The majority of them went to Thailand not to settle permanently but to make their fortune or atleast eke out a living. They are very critical of the freedom and emancipation of Thai women, such an attitude creates psychological barriers and that is one reason that they do not allow their womenfolk freedom, and send their daughters back home for marriage as well as for education.

A comparison of Punjabi women and Gorakhpuri women shows that the status of women in definitely affected by the cultural, contextual and situational factors.

References

Atal,R., 1988: Punjabi's in Thailand. MPhil Dissertation (unpublished). Patiala. Punjab University.

Atal, Y., 1989: Outsiders versus Insiders: The phenomenon of Sandwich Culture. *Sociological Bulletin*, 38 (1).

Bose, P.N., 1927: *The Indian colony of Siam*. Motilal Banarasi Das.

Cadey, J.F., 1964: *South-East Asia: its Historical Development*. New York, McGrow Hill.

1966: *Thailand, Burma, Laos and Cambodia*. New Jersey, Prentice Hall Inc.

Goedes, G., 1966: *The Making of South-east Asia*. London, Routbege and Kegan Paul.

1968: *The Indianized Status of South-East Asia*. Honolulu, East-West Centre Press.

Gupta, S.K., 1999. *Indians in Thailand*. Delhi, India International.

5

Kargil to Khammam: Status of Women in Tribal India

B.R. Rizvi

Time and again the gender questions have moved its way from footnotes to the centre page of writings. Even then the studies on women till recently are being looked as an 'appendage to social research' (Fruzzetti 1990). Whenever any problem or issues regarding woman is being addressed, it is done under the frame of family sociology which represents the pan-Indian society.

The typical Indian family follows the principles of Manu which is based on exercise of authority and power. It may or may not be wielded by a male but it certainly draws its legitimacy with the male line and is derived as well as determined by economic and power relations within the larger society and culture.

To understand the status of woman in tribal India, it is to be seen in terms of the influences and contradictions given by the Indian society. In Indian context we find that here an individual is governed by two principles of the society.

(1) He has some responsibilities to perform by virtue of which he has certain rights from the society,

(2) His position in the society which dictates his responsibilities.

Here an understanding about women in the Brahmanical law becomes necessary to bring the issues on the status of the tribal woman. According to the law the purpose of life of woman was determined by her being the medium for the productions of sons. Manu's code determines that in childhood a female must be subject to her father, in youth to her husband, when her lord is dead to her sons, a woman must never be independent (M. Mueller, *Manu* p.147). Three important factors dominated the marriage law.

(i) Marriage as sacrament and duty
(ii) Marriage age - the stress on per-puberty marriage
(iii) Hypergamy - institutionalised through *anuloma* theory for the preservation of social hierarchy which ultimately gave rise to the institution of dowry. (K.M. Kapadia)

In inheritance of property rights of women can be seen in the light of kinship system based upon the solidarity of paternally related men in inheritance of landed property and continuation of ancestor worship in the male lineage. The ownership right of a man over his wife extended beyond his death to the offspring procreated by another man, mostly his brother with her.

The women were excluded from the right to inherit, only the patrimony was retained and extended. A daughter was excluded from the right of inheritance. She can gain the inheritance right through her son. But she herself could not dispose the property (Max Mulier, *Manu* III). However she will get some ornaments, utensils and clothes as *Sthreedhana* on her marriage. However as a wife she was theoretically the co-owner of the property with the husband which gave her the right of sustenance in the family of her husband. Windows as guardians of minor sons had an indirect share in the property of their husband.

Under this backdrop, few questions can be posed for determining the status of the tribal woman :

(i) the traditional pattern of authority and the nature of resistance if any to the authority;
(ii) marriage laws—social regulations and marital relationship;
(iii) the inheritance and property rights;
(iv) the behavioural norm towards both the sexes;
(v) the economic participation and the labour in home and outside;
(vi) the technological advances and thereby the power structure and
(vii) the role in public arena - political rights.

To explore the above, this paper would like to concentrate on three relationship during the life of a tribal woman within the socio-cultural conditions of the society—as a daughter, as a wife and as a widow.

The observations on the above questions and relationships will be based on author's data generated on Hill Korwa of Surguja (MP), the Balti of Kargil (J & K), the Koya of Khammam (Andhra Pradesh) and the tribes of East Khasi Hills (Meghalaya) at different stretches of his field studies.

Among these the economy of Hill Korwa is centred round the activities of food procurement, i.e., hunting, food gathering, marginal agriculture, animal husbandry and horticultures. Agriculture labour provides livelihood to the landless Korwa. The Khasi tribes are engaged in Swidden cultivation with hoe and follow the matrilineal descent. Both the Koya tribes and Balti tribes are settled agriculture but Balti follow Shiite Islam as religion.

In general, it has been found that the tribes do not have any special preference for boys over the girls. The girls receive as much attention as the boys do in her childhood and infancy may be because of the economic role, the women play in these societies. Among the Khasi society, woman is the embodiment of Khasi matriliny. Only a female is adopted and never a male (Natarajan 1977: 136).

As an economic participant in the society as well as the home maker, the girls training with various chores begins at an early age. She follows her mother in her domestic work, brings fuel from the forest, water from the well. She is expected to look after her younger siblings when her mother is busy in her work. Among Korwa, a girl from her early childhood is conditioned by the society to share the responsibilities of her mother before marriage and of her husband's mother, to whom she treats as her next mother after her marriage. They like the girls to be hardworking astute dancers responsive to their suitors.

In selection of mate the tribal girls enjoy more freedom. Sexual life of Korwa girls starts much before puberty from the age of 8 or 9 years. Acquaintances with boys develop at market, fairs and dancing festivals. Parents however observe the movements and activities of their children. If a boy develops a fancy for a particular girl belonging to another clan, his father seeks the girl for his son for engagement (*mangalsutra*) and agrees to pay bride price (*ma-sari*) demanded by girls father at marriage (*biah*). Premarital sex relation in most societies is not looked down upon provided it does not result in pregnancy. But even than in such cases the child is legitimized by marrying off the girl with some penalty. While negotiating a marriage usually a girl's working capabilities including home management and efficiency in agriculture work brings more bride-price. The services of a daughter is equally important to a tribal family, hence the custom of bride price payable by the groom's family to the girls family of orientation at the time of marriage is just like a compensation for the future loss of her services. In case she is responsible for the dissolution of marriage, the bride price has to be paid back either in part or in full. If she elopes with another man the latter has to regularise the divorce by repaying the brideprice. Here an important point emerges, the economic viability of the woman is challenged through brideprice.

In all the four cases, the economic viability of the woman is the concern for the society Shether it is the patrilineal or matrilineal society. Roy Burman (1978: 24) says that it is the labour power of women that is purchased with bride price. Apart from this the dimension of alliance between the kin groups is taken into consideration. Among the Koya, besides the bride price given in cash, the mother of the bride gets a cow from the groom's side.

A woman begins a new life when she is married. Her role and status gets an importance on being a wife and prospective mother of the children. A clear cut division of labour exists in the family. A woman in expected to work at home attending all the domestic chores and also outside as economic partner. Rizvi (1983) says thc Balti woman's responsibility is not only to procreate and raise the children but to keep the house and hearth warm at 25°C. The winter is a real test for them as during this period a considerable number of male population migrates to the adjoining states to work as wage labourers leaving their woman and children behind. Hence the entire responsibility to run the households during winters lie on the shoulder of Balti women. The women dig the surface of frozen rivers and fetch water from pits dug out with shovels and areas. The cattle are to be tended within the confines of the cattle sheds. The women has to walk at least 10 kms daily to collect low bushes and yak-dung during summers to keep the hearth burning.

Among the Hill Korwa, the economic expertise of women is utilised in day to day life. The males being expert archers and hunters are constantly in need of reed and bamboos from which weapons will be made for hunting. The women play an important role in bringing the raw material from the forest. They are an active food gatherers and their collection consists both edible and non-edible forest produces. The processing and cooking of the collected items are again feminine pursuits.

A tribal women though is expected to be capable to making quick decisions and translating them into swift actions in her home and in economic participation, but from her early years of life, a girl is taught to be sub-missive to authority whether at home or outside and this comes in the way of developing strong opinions and commitment outside her home world. Even among the matrilineal Khasi, there is a proverb saying that "war and politics are for men; while property and children are for women" A Khasi girl should be modest, hard working and obedient to elders, she should never come before them unless she is called for. Next to her husband, a woman is expected to obey her mother-in-low. She is expected to behave in a definite rule of etiquette with her affinal relations. Her motherhood though brings her a special status but it also puts additional burden of work and responsibility. She is expected to resume her normal duties shortly after the birth of the child. As her daughters grow she slowly gets some breathing space. Though in matrilineal tribes the wife decides all the issues concerning the family but she is expected to consult her brothers in all the decisions.

A Korwa individual is entitled to claim the partition of immovable property in the life time of his father but the latter remains to *dejure* owner of the property. A man can become *dejure* owner of the immovable property only after the death of his father or if the latter transfers the ownership to his son by an act of will. Women are not entitled to any share of their fathers property. In case of *gharjawain* marriages, a willing father, however can give a portion of land to his daughter. In such cases when the woman is the owner of the property, the property is inherited by the sons and not by the husband.

A Koya woman in Khammam has no right to inherit the property of her parents or of her husband. Denial of property rights considerably erodes her status in the family. She becomes a burden to her parents who are always eager to receive the amount of brideprice through her marriage. After the marriage of brothers, an unmarried Koya girl lives almost like a stranger in her own home. She earns in order to fulfil her basic needs and to contribute her bit in the family economy. Though a daughter has no right over parental property but she enjoys the right of maintenance from her brother in case the father dies before her marriage. A widow similarly does not enjoy any rights on her deceased husband's property which is either passed on her sons or to the brothers of the deceased husband if she does not have a son.

The Balti girls are entitled for one-third portion of their parental property, though the same is neither demanded nor usually given. They are also entitled for her father's property in full in case of absence of a male sileling. In such case, the girls remain with their parents through *mag-pa* marriage where the husband and his family member do not have the right of inheritance, but his children have the right to inherit their mother's property.

Among the Khasis, the younger daughter known as *ka dhaddah* inherits the lion's share of both ancestral and acquired property of the parents. The elder daughter also inherits a portion of such property but the sons expect among the war Khasis are deprived of the ancestral property. Although the younger daughter inherits the property she is not the sole owner. She merely acts as its custodian and hence known as *ka nongri da nong sumar.* It is the maternal uncle who has the actual control over the property. (Valentina Pakyntein 19.., Gurdon 1975 : Natarajan 1977). The maternal uncle (Vkn) and the youngest daughter act as the family priest and priestess for performing rituals pertaining to the family (Synrem 1986). It is also the duty of the youngest daughter to see that the death rites of her family members are performed in an appropriate manner. She is responsible for all the members of the family. She resides in her mothers house and look after her parents in their old age. (Gurdon : 76-85, Natarajan 1977 : 18, War 1988: 4, Syiem 1988: 4). She also looks after her unmarried and disabled brothers and sisters, widowed, divorced or deceased sister and brothers family and also their children. Her house is regarded by all family members who are in need (Syiem 1988: 3,4). She performs these responsibilities under the guidance of her maternal uncle and thus the rights of inheritance exist collaterally with the socio-economic and socio-religious responsibilities.

Rizvi (1988) in his study on the marriage system in the Kargil area found the existence of short contract marriage *nikah-e-ingatai* or *mutah* quite high. The duration of contract varied between 20 years to 100 years and the price of *mehr* is relatively low, ranging between, Rs. 28 to Rs.100. *Mutah* qualifies a man to marry a woman of his choice for a stipulated period of time. The marriage alliance in this case is terminated at the will of male spouse after the payment of *mehr*. In such case the woman and the children fathered by them are at his mercy.

Discussion

In the previous pages, we came across the tribes at different levels of economy, i.e., from the food gathering stage to swidden cultivation and settled agriculture. Three tribes follow the patrilineal system of social organisation and the remaining one follow matrilineal system. The study shows that the tribal woman are no more different from the rest of woman's world. We find she has to follow certain expected norm of behaviour, her rights and duties are different from that of menfolk. She is considered as an economic asset and her life is surrounded by the activities of domestic chores, raising children and working in the field. But her economic participation does not give her a high status in her community. Her participation in the working force is higher but it has been found that the improved technology in the agricultural sphere, right from the hunting-gathering stage to settled agriculture, there has been an increase in the workload on the workforce of the woman. Also the responsibility of feeding the family members has increased but the males have enjoyed the gains from the technological advance. In many of cases, it has been found that either the males indulge themselves in alcohol or if they find increase in the woman power, they try to neutralise their power by blaming them indulging in witchcraftism. In many cases the apathy towards the woman have also made them alieniated from their own community.

What we find in a Khasi family, the mother is the owner of the property and her brother holds the authority in the family. This brother, though after his marriage shifts to his wife's natal family, exercises his authority at his own natal family. Bareh (1964) says that among the Khasi, the woman is *ka Nongrilang,* i.e., in keeper, (custodian or trustee) of the house, the man - U Rangbah Uba Da (protector). He has the honoured position, he is U knii, i.e., maternal uncle (counsellor) to his nephew and nices, he is Ukpa (the father) at his wife's home. Thus though the management of land and property is at the hand of women, the social and political contri is taken over by the men. Thus though she looks after the management but she is kept away from the decision making process. The Khasi women are completely kept away from taking any part in the political affairs. Though the descent is through female line, a woman can never become the head of the state. In most of the cases the tribal woman can never hold the post of the religious office. Among Koya, the office of Samuta Poya, Pedda Patel are hereditary and pass to eldest male issue in keeping with the law of primogeniture. Even the *pujari* or priest and witch doctor is always a male.

It has been observed that in spite of their active economic participation, the women have virtually no right to inherit the land and immovable property. Among the Koya's of Khammam, the rule of inheritance of property favours the male members. This has pushed their women folk, especially the widow and spinsters, towards wage employment. The rule of inheritance shows that even after marriage the woman are not entitled to inherit their husbands property. More over, the addiction of Koya men to toddy and liquor has given rise to perpetual maltreatment of women and the breakdown of matrimonial ties. The area is a major producer of cash crops, i.e., chill and tobacco. Having ample job opportunities around the Koya girls feel hesitant to bear the rigours of married life. With the supply of cash money which they earn through labour activities, they want to lead an independent and carefree life. The Koya female workers thus came into contact with non-Koya and adopted system of values which is entirely different from their own. Gradually a process of alienation from their society has set in. Economically they are not dependent on their parents and guardians but the economic independence is bringing individualistic attitude in them and on this point they can reject marriage alliances being proposed or negotiated by their parents. This process of alienation has posed a danger of disintegration of the institution of family.

The following case study of a Kaya girl of Murmur colony (Khammam) will help in bringing the above points clearer. Gatpil Muttle (25), the daughter of Gatpil Mallaiah of Murmur colony is a labourer with Roads and Building Division of Public Works Department. Her employer's trolly-tractor would reach in the village early in the morning to pick up her and other labourers from the village. She would return home in the afternoon to take meals. After half an hour she will again return to the place of work. She will return before the dusk and set listlessly in the outer verandah. Even her small siblings, a two years old girl and a 5 year old boy playing around, falling down and crying will neither attract her attention nor stir her feelings. After sitting and taking an hour's rest she will visit her friends in the village one by one till midnight. Then she would come, spread the bamboo mat in the verandah and sleep. Thursday is a closed day for her she will have to go to Venkatapuram because it is a day for weekly market. She will start 11 kms. journey early in the morning with her girl companions, do the shopping from her savings and return in the afternoon by 5 o'clock if she can resist the temptation of seeing a Telugu movie. In case she decides to see the movie, she will start her journey back to home at 11 o'clock in the night reaching at the destination well after midnight too tired to speak or even to take meals.

In her entire schedule of work Gatpil Mutti has no or very little time to play with her siblings, assist her mother in the household chores or participate in village affairs whether it is a marriage or any other festive occasion. Her parents have virtually lost control on her because she is a working hand and contributes to family earning. Even if she opts to marry a non tribal, neither her parents nor the Kulam panchayat will be major impediment to her designs. She has saved sufficient money to pay *mongali thappu* to the Kulam panchayat. This case is not an exception, Gatpil Mutti represents a category of Koya girls who find themselves full or pretty alienated from the rest of their society.

Thus, the Koya rule of inheritance, culture contact, modernity as well as passive role of the Kulam panchayat plays a major role into the disintegration of Koya family institution and four distinct categories of Koya woman emerges on the scene:

(i) the traditionally married self-employed housewives as per Koya value system and world view;

(ii) the alienated women - either married or living with non-tribals. After paying *mognali thappu* to the Kulam panchayat, they have little or no interaction with their own group;

(iii) the traditional spinsters, whose main source of livelihood is through wage labour, are in search of Koya husbands who treat them kindly and do not maltreat them;

(iv) Rebellious spinsters who stoutly refuse to have a marital alliance with Koya boys.

Thus, the above discussion brings us to conclude that the neither the economic participation and status nor the control over the property does help to enhance the status of tribal women. Rather it is the systematic arrangement based on division of labour for the continuity of the society. Also in the recent years it was felt that the powers and responsibilities to make plans and take decision regarding the various programmes at panchayat level should be given to the women through the 73rd Constitutional Amendment Act, Article 15(3). But in most of the cases in the tribal and rural areas the women's voice is not heard rather it is still the male who speak for the women.

In all kinds of society, whether tribal or non-tribal, it is found that two related issues are concerned with the status of women—one is the attitude based on beliefs and values and depends on the socialization process and the values on women's role and duties. And the other is directly related to legal stirctures or *dharmshashtras*. These two combine to form the position and status of women in the society. The ignorance of their rights whether political, socio-economic combined with illiteracy leads to th exploitation of women and their inability to form a pressure group. The benefits can only be accrued if they take up their own cause not only as a gender issue but also as a human being and work unitedly for their educational, economic and social empowerment.

References

Altekar, A.S., 1956: *The Position of Women in Hindu Civilization*, Benaras.

Bareh, Hamlet, 1964: *Khas Democracy*. Shillong.

Fruzzetti, Lina, 1990: *The Gift of a Virgin, 'Women, marriage and Ritual in a Bengali Society*. New Delhi: Oxford University Press.

Max Muller, Rpt., 1967: The Sacred Books of the East (SBE) : The Laws of Manu: translated by G. Buhler, Delhi.

Misra, P.K., B.R. Rizvi and S.B. Chakroborty, 1993: Tribal Customary Law in southern India, in *Tribal Ethnography, Customary Law and Change*. K.S. Singh (Ed.) New Delhi: Concept.

Makhopadhyay, K., 1998: Dynamics of Ethnic Identity Maintenance among the Khashi of North East India in *North East India Elthno Cultural Perspective and Process A.K. Danda et. al.* (Ed.) Calcutta: The Indian Anthropological Society.

Natarajan, N., 1977: Missionaries among the Khashi. Delhi: Sterling Publications:

Pakyntein, Valentina, 1999: Gender Preference in Khashi society in *Wonder that is Culture* T.B. Subba (Ed.) New Delhi: Mittal Publications.

Rizvi, B.R., 1977: Koya Customary Laws—Law and Justice in a tribe of South Central India. Unpublished report submitted in Anthropological Survey of India.

1978: "Role of Women in Tribal Economy : A Study of the Hill Korwa of Surguja" in *Tribal Women in India*, Calcutta : Indian Anthropological Society.

1988: "Temproary Contract Marriage System among the Muslims of Kargil (J&K)" in *Marriage in India*. B.B. Goswami *et. al.* (Ed.) Calcutta : Anthroplogical Survey of India.

1989: *Hill Korwas of Chattisgarh - A Study of Tribal Economy*. New Delhi : Gyan Publishing House.

1993: *The Balti - A Scheduled Tribe of Jammu & Kashmir*. New Delhi : Gyan Publishing House.

1995: The Other Half : A Study of Muslim Tribal Women of Kargil (Jammu & Kashmir. Unpublished paper)

Roy Burman, B.K., 1978: "Emerging Humanity and Tribal Woman in India" in *Tribal Women in India*. Calcutta Indian Anthropological Society.

Syiem, I.M., 1988: Women in Khasi Society : Seminar on Status of Women in Tribal Cultural of Meghalaya Organised by Centre for Literary and Cultural Studies, NEHU, 13-14 July.

Synrem, H.K., 1986: Revivalism, in the Khasi Society/unpublished Ph.D. Dissertation. NEHU.

War, J., 1988: Status of women in traditional Khasi culture: Seminar on Status of women in Tribal cultures of Meghalaya organised by Centre for Literary and Cultural Studies, NEHU, 13-14 July.

6

Maternal and Child Health Care in Relation to Literacy in Bharias—A Primitive Tribe of Madhya Pradesh

G.D. Pandey

Introduction

With the advent of Fifth Five Year Plan, a fresh diagnosis was made to adopt a new strategy for the develcpment of the tribal community in general and tribal communities living a secluded life in particular, such primitive tribes were identified by considering apart from economic criterion, some more distinguished features like level of literacy, remoteness and near stagnant population. Out of 52 primitive tribes identified in our country out two belonged to the state of Madhya Pradesh. Bharias of Patalkot Valley is one of them.

Maternal and child health services for tribal population has remained largely neglected (Basu *et al* 1994). Nevertheless, the consistent plea of health planners for improving health services for tribal mothers and children has resulted in several programmes which however implemented with varying degrees of success due to traditional practices, taboos and other barriers (Pandey and Tiwary 1993), Pandey *et al*, 1996; Pandey and Saxena, 1998; Kar, 1993 and Derarapallu, 1992). The acceptability of health care facilities among the primitive tribes has been lowest. One of the reasons may be the high illiteracy prevailing in these tribes. This paper is an endeavour to study knowledge, attitude and practices of maternal and child health care in relation to literacy level of the Bharie couple.

The People

Bharias are one of the smaller tribal groups of Madhya Pradesh. They refer to call themselves Bhumia. It is a Dravidian tribe residing principally in the central region of Madhya Pradesh. As small section of this community lives in an area known as Patalkot in Chhindwada district. This area is a deep depression in the hilly region, where the approach being extremely difficult. This group has been by passed by modern development because of the physical situation of their habitat. The Bharias living inside valley has been accorded status of primitive tribe by the government of India.

The Data

The Regional Medical Research Centre for Tribals, Jabalpur has collected information on socio-demographic characteristics of the Bharias of Patalkot Valley during 1995-97. The data were collected with the help of questionnaire and personal interview. The study included 144 Bharia households consisting of 132 eligible couples (aged below 50 years).

Results

The data analysed on socio-demographic characteristics have been show in Table 6. It appears that about half of the households were nuclear (50.3 per cent) Sixty-two per cent households were electrified. Two-third households earned their livelihood from agriculture and forest produce. Not a single household was found having service as main occupation. About 22 per cent population were found literate. The annual household income was Rs. 6317 only. The mean age at marriage for the females was 15.8 years. The total fertility rate was 4.7 and age at first birth was 20.5 years. Out of 132 husbands, only 42 were found to be literate. Since, very few eligible females were found literate (2.2 per cent) the analysis of maternal and child health care has been carried out only with the literate husbands.

Antenatal Care

As evident from Table 6.3, 19 per cent of the wives of literate husbands received antenatal care compared to only 11 per cent among the illiterate husbands. More Bharia wives of illiterate husbands avoided looking foods like Kodo, Juar, Balhar, etc. as these were considered cold foods during pregnancy.

More changes (42.8 per cent) occurred in social behaviour among the wives of literate husbands during pregnancy period whereas only 16.7 per cent wives of the literate husbands stopped physical activities during this period. This indicates larger participation of women in workforce. However, when the Chi^2 test is applied significant difference is noticed only in case of abstaining from physical activities during pregnancy.

Delivery Care

It can be observed from Table 6.4 that services of trained *dais* (16.7 per cent) were availed more by the wives of literate husbands compared to the wives of illiterate husbands. To cut the naval cord majority of the wives used sickle (70 per cent) in case of the wives of illiterate husbands, while wives of literate husbands favoured old blade (42.8 per cent). As regard material applied on the stump, though, 97 per cent wives of illiterate husbands applied powder of matka/khapara or area nut, 88 per cent wives of the literate husbands applied the same. As this table is quite self-explanatory it needs no further description.

Post-natal Care

It is observed from Table 6.5 that higher percentage of wives of literate husbands used soap for cleaning the mother and the child after delivery compared to the wives of illiterate husbands. This difference is statistically significant. It may be noted that wives of literate husbands started breast feeding on the same day after the delivery and shows lesser tendency of discarding colostrum. A higher percentage of wives of literate husbands took bath with soap. This factor has also been found to be associated with the literacy of the husband.

Family Planning

More than fifty-two per cent literate husbands had knowledge of family planning compare to only 22 per cent among the illiterates. Among the illiterates husbands, all of them who claimed to have knowledge, had knowledge of only permanent methods while seven per cent literate husbands also had knowledge of temporary methods, like Nirodh, oral pills. The opinion of literate husbands were more favourable towards family planning. Near about thirty-five per cent near about of them were of the view that family planning keeps family small, though, 21 per cent were also of the view that operation was harmful to health. A higher percentage of couples where husbands were literate were found adopters of family planning (14.3 per cent) while only 3.3 per cent couples were adopters in the illiterate group (Table 6.6).

Discussion

The study has clearly indicated that literacy had played a positive role to change traditional customs regarding antenatal care, care during delivery and postnatal care and has provided better understanding towards family planning among the Bharias. Changes are significant in case of food avoidance during pregnancy, stopping of physical activities, instrument used to cut the naval cord, use of soap for bathing of child and mother and discard of colostrum. Significant change has been also observed regarding knowledge of family planning and opinion about family planning. The changes would have been speedier if the wives were also educated. The study lays stress on the need of encouraging literacy in the tribe more specifically the female literacy. The higher literacy will encourage better understanding of hygienic habits, acceptability of modern MCH services and reduction of infant and maternal mortality in this tribe which are highly prevailing in central India.

TABLE-6.1
SOCIO-ECONOMIC INDICATORS OF THE TRIBE

Type of H.H. (%)	*N = 144*
Nuclear	50.3
Joint	49.7
Electrified Houses	61.5
Occupation	
Agriculture	30.6
Collection of forest Produce	37.4
Labour	33.0
Service	0.0
Possession of land per acre	5.2
Literacy (%)	
M	34.1
F	8.9
T	21.5
Annual Income	Rs. 6317

TABLE-6.2
AGE-SEX STRUCTURE AND RELATED INDICES

Age	
0-14	40.0
15-59	53.8
60+	6.2
YDR (%)	75.5
ODR (%)	11.5
Total Dependency Ratio	87.0
Index of Ageing	15.5

(Contd.)

(Contd.)

Age	
Sex Ratio	1068
Age at Marriage	
M	18.1
F	15.8
Consanguinity	55.3
Marital distance	10.2

YDR = Young dependency ratio
ODR = Old dependency ratio

TABLE-6.3
ANTENATAL CARE ACCORDING TO LITERACY OF HUSBAND

		Literate (N = 42)	*Illiterate (N = 90)*	χ^2 *Values*
1.	Antenatal services Received			
	Yes	19.0	11.1	
				1.5
	No	81.0	88.9	
2.	Food Avoided			
	Yes	14.3	30.0	
				3.7
	No	85.7	70.0	
3.	Change in Social Activities			
	Yes	42.8	36.6	
				0.5
	No	57.2	63.4	
4.	Stop physical activities			
	Yes	16.7	0.0	

				18.0*
	No	83.3	100.0	
5.	Rest	38.1	36.6	
				1.3
		61.9	63.4	

TABLE-6.4

DELIVERY CARE ACCORDING TO LITERACY OF HUSBAND

	Literate (N = 42)	*Illiterate (N = 90)*	*X^2 Values*
Preparation per cent for delivery	47.6	35.5	2.26
	52.4	74.5	
Eating and drinking before delivery			
Tea	42.8	25.5	1.28
Nothing	57.2	74.5	
Delivery conducted			
Elderly lady	83.3	88.9	0.19
Trained Dai	16.7	11.1	
Delivery posture			
Sitting	95.2	85.5	1.11
Lying	4.8	14.5	
Cord cut by			
Axe	4.7	0.0	*
Sickle	30.9	70.0	13.9
Old blade	42.8	13.4	
New blade	21.6	16.6	(d f = 1)
Preparation applied			
Powder Matka or Khapara	83.3	70.0	*
Areca nut> Powder	4.8	26.7	87.0
Nothing	11.9	3.3	

TABLE-6.5
POST NATAL CARE ACCORDING TO LITERACY OF HUSBAND

For Child	*Literate (N = 42)*	*Illiterate (N = 90)*	*x^2 Values*
(i) Bath with water, soap and massage with mustard oil	57.1	25.6	4.9*
(ii) Bath with warm water and massage mustard oil	42.9	74.4	
Breast Feeding started			
Same day	100.0	96.7	0.7
After 2 days	0.0	3.3	
Colostrum discarded			
Yes	4.8	16.7	1.7
No	95.2	83.3	
For Mother			
Bath with warm water and soap	57.1	25.6	4.9*
Bath with only warm water	42.9	74.4	

TABLE-6.6
KAP OF FAMILY PLANNING BY LITERACY OF HUSBAND

Family Planning	*Literate (N = 42)*	*Illiterate (N = 90)*
Knowledge about FP	52.4	22.2
No knowledge of FP	47.6	77.8
Permanent Method		
VT	28.6	5.2
T T	77.1	4.2
VT and TT	14.3	12.2
Temporary Method		
Condom	4.7	0.0
Tab	2.3	0.0
Opinion about FP		
(1) It makes family small	34.6	7.7
(2) Operation harmful to health	21.4	15.5
(3) No Idea	44.0	76.8
Practice		
Yes	14.3	3.3
No	85.7	96.7
Decision taken by		
Husband and wife	9.5	0.0
Husband	90.5	100.0
If Yes		
VT	11.9	2.2
T T	2.4	1.1
Control Tab	0.0	0.0

References

Basu S., A. Jindal and G.Kshatriya, 1994: Perception of health and pattern of health seeking behaviour among the selected tribal population groups of Madhya Pradesh. In: *Tribal Health in India*. S. Basu (Ed). Delhi, Mayank Publications.

Derapallu, J., 1992: Maternal care and obstetric practice among the Konda Dara Tribe. *The Journal of Family Welfare*, 38 (4): 37-44.

Pandey, G.D. and R.S.Tiwary, 1993: Socio-cultural characteristics and health seeking behaviour of the Hill Korwas.

The Journal of Family Welfare, 39 (II): 44-47.

Pandey, G.D. and B.N Saxena, 1988: Distrct level Planning for health and family welfare for the tribals. *Demography India*, 17 (2): 216-223.

Pandey, G.D., J. Roy and R.S. Tiwary, 1996: Socio-cultural charaet ristics and health seeking behaviour of the Khairwars of Madhya Padesh. *The Journal of Family Welfare*, 42(2): 49-54.

Kar, P.K., 1993: Reproductive health behaviour of the Nocte Women in Arunachal Pradesh. *Social Change*, 23 (4): 40-45.

7

Status of Women in Rural Jharkhand

A.N. Sandhwar

Even after more than 50 years of Independence positive spell of modernization and industrialization, development of Science and Technology, entering into space and nuclear age, we are still talking about status of women. What a contradiction? At one end so much scientific advancement and on another hand still continuation of age old socially and culturally embedded stigma on the women. For understanding of the affairs of women and their position, we must look into the fact what different persons have said about the position of women which reflect status of women in a society. Female as a matter of fact in any society suppose to have equal status and right in every sphere, even though nature has made this class physically weak. Culturally then are considered as weak and second class citizen of society, so, their sufferings are in many folds in spite of safeguards provided by enactment of different acts, i.e., dowry death, rape, discrimination, eve teasing, physical and mental torture, etc. Different social thinkers have expressed their opinions about women.

According to G.C. Paejatter "Man is active and independent, women—passive and dependent".

Napolean Bonapart expressed that "what a mad idea for

demand of equality for women with that of men. Women are nothing but a machine for producing children."

Lord Tennesion Alfred considered "man for the field and women for the hearth, man to command and women to obey."

"Devi Bhagwat declared—women are this friends nor foes."

Ramchaaritra Manas—drums, low caste (Shudra), animals and women are subject to torture *(Dhol, Shudra, Pasn and Nari-eye sub hai taran ke adhikari)*, only then they can be brought to right path.

The Christian Bible declare—"how women can be clean."

The Jain philosophy propagates—do not desire women as they constantly change their mind."

Thus, we see that such statements depict the very low status of women in a society. They have tried to establish that women are "expendable assets".

The finding of UNESCO report revealed that "women starve more than man". If there is illiteracy, "women are more illiterate than men."

The WHO reported that in most parts of India "Girls are effected by severe mal-nutrition".

At different times women have been socially, economically, physically and psychologically subjected to exploitations though-out the history. Unfortunately it is still continuing in rural areas. The urban areas are also affected in less degree due to increase in education, modernization and industrialization.

Rural Jharkhand area is a mosaic of different levels of population, religion and economy. Even today among the Hindus, cases of child marriage, no value of their wishes for marriage and keep very low position in the family. Women belonging to low caste are kept as.......(elicit sexual relationship) by Thakurs and Zagirdars. In rural Jharkhand, their is conceptualized system of *Nachni-*

Pratha mostly found in Gumla areas. Under this *Pratha* a woman is kept as *Nachni* by economically affluent people and keep sexual relationship without marriage. She has to obey his master in all respects. Women have no rule in political organisation as well as in the major family decision and in making of the budget.

Among the Muslim community they have some liberties but a male can have 3 wives at a time and can give divorce very easily just saying ***Talak, Talak and Talak.*** A Muslim woman to produce children even if she has poor health as no family planning system is adopted. She cannot be Mullaha in the mosque. It is still continuing and all these show lower status of women.

In Christian society even today cannot address the Church in spite of education, impact of urbanization, modernization and industrialization.

Among the tribals, the situation is comparatively better, and possess higher status. The girls marry of their own choice. Bride price is paid to them. But they work much hard in domestic works, in the field and other economic activities. As a matter of fact a women work much more than males. The traditional *Panchyat* believe the saying of a woman in case of illicit sexual relationship, etc., if a girl becomes pregnant and on her saying the boy is forced to marry her, although pre-marital and extra-marital relationship is practiced and is accepted in the society.

But under the customary law women has no right of inheritance of property either from father or husband. Unmarried daughters or widows get *Khorposh* for their maintenance. After death or remarriage/marriage it goes to other family male members.

It shows the lower status of women. In recent days cases of rape, dowry death and physical exploitation have gone up in rural areas. Female belonging to 4 years to 70 years of age are reported being raped. Similar is the case of dowry death.

Dian-Pratha is another black shot in rural society. Concept of *Dian* is misnomer, and far away from the reality. It is based upon false believe that an elderlywoman has become *dian* and she eats the child or any member of the family. In return she is beaten, physically tortured and even murdered. Cases of *Dian* frequently appears in the newspapers. It is reported that issue-less and elderly women (above 70 years) are murdered to capture his property.

It is most unfortunate and tragic scenario of our society. So many acts for safeguard of women have been enacted, i.e., Article 44 (Articles 41, 42 and 43 say that women should be given special social security, to give more education with a view to provide more employment).

- Article 325—under this act male and female have been provided equal rights in electoral rolls and there should be no discrimination.
- 74 Amendments—special arrangement for women representation in local administration.
- Hindu Marriage Act' 1953—under this act a male can't have second wife unless previous is divorced or dead.
- 1956—Act banning the prostitution.
- Child Marriage Act 1860—child marriage is a crime, 1829 age of marriage of boy 21 and girl-18.
- 1990—Tribal Management Act under it special provisions given to women.

It is a sad plight that in spite of several steps taken to raise the status of women but still is deplorable as tradition die hard and no radical changes appear. This is why even after more than 50 years of independence and so many efforts made by different organisations, still the status of women is very low and they are faced with brutal torture and exploitation. There is a need of effective measures to tackle the problem of women can save women themselves. They have to make efforts in this direction.

8

Status of Woman in Maria Society

V.D. Jha

Bastar district, located in the south eastern corner of M.P. covers an area of 39,176 sq. kms. Till recently, it was known as *CUL DE SAC* and *TERRA INCOGNITA*. The region remained isolated due to its physical relief and paucity of means of communication. The tribes inhibiting this vast hilly country have retained their primitive culture.

The Marias, occupying the Jagdalpura, Dantewar, Narayanpur, Bijapur, and Konta tahsils of Bastar district have been divided into two groups, i.e., the Hill Marias and the Plain Marias. The Hill Marias, reside in the region in which a chain of hills extends in an area of about 1456 sq. kms. Prior to the recently introduced forest roads from Orchha to Kutul and from Narayanpur to Kohkameta it was practically inaccessible. The Hill Marias are least affected from the wave of modern civilization.

At the very outset I would express that the Maria woman, specially the Abujhmaria enjoys, tremendous liberty and higher status than man in the society.

She has practically no bondaze in pre-marital social life excepting that she is not allowed to marry in her father's clan.

The Marias strictly follow the rules of exogamy. The female

is allowed to participate in every social ceremony. Maria girl cannot be compelled to marry against her wishes. Furthermore, Maria woman is allowed to abandon her husband, of course, with the approval of the village Panchayat. Grigson's observation that practically "no girl in Abujhmaria preserves her virginity till marriage and no value is set on pre-marital chastity" is not acceptable. As a matter of fact, pre-marital sexual relationship is tolerated and no serious action is taken by the community. But, certainly such act is looked down upon.

However, it is remarkable that an unmarried girl cannot be exploited deceived by any male. In case of pre-marital pregnancy the girl, accompanied by her parents, catches hold of the hands of the responsible boy and the community compels him to marry, the girl. In this context, I would like to mention about *Ghotul* the youth dormitories, about which scholars have expressed variegated opinion.

Though adult Maria girls and boys are allowed in Ghotul, but certainly it is not an institution where they freely involve in sexual relations. Ghotul in fact, is a place where the youngers learn about dance, sing, folk-telling, craft and community rituals. Of course they develop personal likings for each other and later get married with the approval of the community. Ghotul inhabitants assist the village in case of emergency.

Only boys sleep in Ghotuls located in Abujhmarh. Girls are never allowed. The reason behind this is that every village in Abujhmarh, is uniclan. Marriage between the same clan is a taboo. Hence, the community do not take any risk in providing an opportunity to the young boys and girls in getting closely mixed.

There are various checks and don't's on the woman so far as religious ceremonies are concerned. She is not allowed to enter the hedge-temple, eat the sacrificial meals, visit the cremation ground and sleep out in the field when the crops are ripening. During the first menstruation the girl is regarded as excommunicated and readmitted in the community after some ceremonies are performed. Probably, it is done to induce fertility in her. The woman is forced to live in isolation after every menstruation period. It is noteworthy that, the community takes every care of the girl during this period by sending an old woman to lookafter her necessary needs. In some villages their is a common menstruation hut located at some distance from the village.

Immediately after delivery the women lives practically in isolation. Her husband, who cooks food for the wife, is treated as excommunicated during this period for 7 days. The purpose behind such custom is that, the husband should take every care of his wife when she is in need. It exhibits the high status of woman in Maria society. The Abujhmaria is very proud of his woman. Mutual respect between the wife and husband is observed. The woman participates even in the hunting ceremony known as Beech Pandulm. She works in the cultivation field, collects fuel and forest produce. *Purda* and *Sati* system do not prevail in Maria society. Remarriage and widow marriage is allowed. A widow lives in the village of his dead husband, until she marries again. She is never allowed to marry the elder brother of her late husband and a man whom she could not have taken as her husband. The idea behind such restriction is to place checks on the possibility of social crime. The arrange marriage, marriage by exchange and by capture is prevalent. Bride-price is paid in marriage. One who is unable to pay bride-price serves his future father-in-law as suitor-servant for few years. The bride-price in the form of money, grains and clothes, etc. are given to girl's mother. Scholors have expressed that its a sealing of the contract, or compensation on a purchase price. I feel that, its a sort of gratitude expressed by the father of the bridegroom towards the bride's mother for giving the hands of the daughter in marriage. This again exhibits higher status of woman. It may be mentioned that, birth of a son is not treated as special case for joy. The independent status of woman is maintained by the society. The boys sets up his own hut immediately after marriage and stays independently. Hence, the married woman escapes from the furry of the atrocities of her husband's family members.

Though polygamy is allowed but, only one marriage is permitted. A male can keep more woman but the kepts do not get that respect in the society.

Divorce is rarely reported. Adultery is not tolerated.

Marias, specially the Abujhmaria's, attitude towards life is very realistic. They believe in spirits and reincarnation. Majority of the Marias are uneducated.

Change has been marked recently due to the development of means of communications, education and industrialisation. The assimilation in the Hindu fold is in work because of Marias' intimate contacts with the former. The change in costumes of Maria women in the plains has been marked. They are being exploited to some extent by the outsiders. Fortunately, the change is external. Because the Maria adhers to his rituals and religion his soul has not been effected. On the other hand, a strict adherence to the religion and rituals has been marked in the recent past.

9

Employment for Women and Probable Encounters : A Perspective of Home Science

Harapriya Samanataraya

That the statement "women are dependents and therefore can not do most of the works that men do" has been proved to be wrong to a great extent. Equality, liberty and freedom question for women by and large remain at the individual perspective. The hither to dominated position of woman by man has been attributed to her limited scope of entry, ownership and use of resources vital for qualitative living in human civilisation. It is known to all of us that women keep on themselves engaged in home fronts and outside for remunerative jobs. She is not getting relieved from household duties for certain inbuilt socio-cultural mechanism and some ideological reasons .She has been symbolised to be a status occupant of lesser importance throughout the *rite-de-passage* .In the history of humankind somewhere men had assumed the role of protectors and food providers due to favourable circumstances and the women who were once identified as the inventors of agriculture practices, domestication of animals and fire and managers of human resources have been gradually relegated to a subordinated position. Later, the male dominated ideology and socio-cultural practices had systematically alienated her from rights-of freedom of expression and restricted her to the household responsibilities and duties so that she cannot have the scope to look forward for alternatives. The social control mechanisms in due course of time were crafted such that they cannot escape from the andro-centric social 'norms'. Due to the perpetuation of such norms women are being encountering and apprehensive of being encountered with new forms of problems in their occupational frontiers in our changing world. There is asymmetry between men and women in public management in terms of opportunity, power and numbers world over (Guy 1993). Their representation in decision making positions are disproportionately low compared to their opposite gender. Whatever employment available for women are mostly favour the traditional pattern coinciding with the prerogatives. The techno-economic changes, however, is supposed to have opened new vistas for women employment and liberate them from some of the socio-economic bondages.

In our society there were limited job opportunities for women till recently. With the technological revolution and increasing female literacy the women in job markets are increasing day by day. With the advent of information technology and other forms of technological transformations some new out-lets for women have surfaced. In a few cases she was forced to take up outside jobs and in some she opted for challenging jobs. Since she has been represented in all socio-economic classes she encounters different problems depending upon the nature of job.

In this article, the author would like to present her views on the status of women through few data extracted from news clippings. After making a preliminary attempt in describing the status of women in our contemporary society with the career options in general the author wishes to offer her perception on a few encounters that women have in job frontiers and few gender oriented problems at place of work and at home.

Women, since the feudal period have been treated no less than slaves. For centuries she remained subordinate to man and a part of the cultural norm she remained under the *pardah* for many years. Her traditional roles remained confined to house-keeping and rearing the children and dependent aged. Self-expression had been a dream for her. Her scope for grievance ventilation was the husband or the close female kin or friend . She was not having the freedom of education, property rights, and other forms of economic and political powers. In traditional Indian families the male elders while mitigating the family strives, often between the mother-in-law and the daughter-in law, often pass the statement before the members of the family that neither the mother nor the daughter in law belong to our family. They have come from other family hence they are expected to have less involvement for the family status. This implies that the male in his family conflict management impute female as the guilt and hardly go for the relational scanning process between the genders. Thus she is projected as sources of family disorganisation.

Women irrespective of class have been catering the needs of men in the family and outside. Even in contemporary society the incoming of a new female member by birth is not considered as a joyful event. However, among the affluent and upper middle class families due to small family norms for many it is being tolerated and rationalised. The urge for a male child does not eliminate from the mind of such parents. It seems that the principle of gender equality has been enshrined in Indian Constitution, fundamental rights, and directive principles and so also in the preamble of human rights charter. To have the equal treatment for women in our contemporary society still it remained a far cry. Her image in the society can easily be correlated with events of foeticide, girl child abuse, maternal mortality and morbidity, dowry and other forms of menace. The advertiser project her gestures and postures to market their products and thereby the woman in market scenario is identified as human forms without human contents.

In a recent comparative sample study on working women and non-working women in Trivandrum Radha Devi and Ravindran from IIPS Bombay have stated that working women manage to do their household works in lesser time by increasing their efficiency or lessen their burden by getting help from others including the husbands, however, the relationship between expectation of help from husband and the actual help provided by husband is not clear (1985). With regard to the women labour participation in informal sector similarly a few authors are of opinion that the problems encountered women is less known and therefore special attention in this area of research should be given such that the findings will have a contribution for the policy planning and administration (Majumdar 1977, D'Souza 1980, Majumdar 1983, and Dighe 1985). There are few who stated that women in general experience fewer obstacles in gaining promotion today than ever before (Mishra, Vardhan, Kavita and Mishra 1986). Seth in the recent book on Women in India has analysed the ıeason of women getting prevented from acquiring the benefits that they deserve as on near half of the population of India. She has traced status of women from the Vedic age downwards and conclude that women themselves do not want confrontation but justice (2001).

In our culture in India woman has been venerated as mother who sacrifices her life for the sake of children. The socialisation that starts from home is in real sense a matri-centric. It is a cultural output wherein the child imitates mother more than any of the interacting person during the first three years. Since the psychic foundation is shaped by mother anything gone wrong is attributed to the careless socialisation of the mother and the reverse is normally appropriated by the father. At home and outside they have to do family need based works of which almost the whole is centred around the husband and/or the progeny. They are denied of freedom of expression, education and economic power to a large extent. A few statistical data would give us a picture.as to what extent the women are sharing power equal to men.

For last many decades the male-female ratio in India has never been encouraging rather the declining trend of sex ratio has already alarmed the country. Their representation also revealed the same. 49 out of 545 parliamentary seats are held by women; out of 25 judges in Supreme Court there is only one women ;only 3 per cent of the total Orissa High Court judges are women, and 9.9 per cent and 2.2 per cent of the total are represented as IAS and IPS respectively. According to Human Development Report the status of women is closely related to their active participation in decision making processes. In sense the extent of such participation may be referred to as her empowerment. The recently held 4th world conference at Bejing in Sept. 1999 the emphasis was given to equalise the opportunities and status. The laws and regulation in favour of women may be many. All those have meaning only when they get public approval and people who matter internalise these in right perspectives.

In India the macro level studies revealed that the .data on women participation in economy and labour force is distorted. The important reason for this may be attributed to the data collection process where the male headed household ignores the information on female. For example D'Souza notes that "cultural and social stereotypes regarding the concept of head of the household has given rise to unreliable data and serious under reporting of economic contribution of women in agriculture and in the informal urban sector (1980).

The last census reports have indicated a positive shift for female participation in economically productive works compared to its previous periods. Their distribution in cultivation, agricultural labourers, in household industries repair works, works in coir and *bidi* factory, lace factory, brick-making industries, trade, commerce, business, transport, construction works, office assistants in hotels, motels and restaurants, sales persons in shops, engagement in local-self governments as the regular employees, daily wage worker not figuring in pay rolls of the office of the private and the public sectors, employees with their respective pay rolls in State and central government organisations and so on. The general trend marked in the change in the pattern of women's work participation in various occupational categories is attributes to the mushroom growth of institutions both in rural and urban sectors. The taste of the people has changed. For example to take food outside in week ends and in other occasions has created demand for quick food services units which has engaged a few females. The growth of institutions like banks, hospitals, schools offices and other private processing units in rural and urban areas have also created job opportunities for the females.

The technological outgrowth of electronic, electrical and mechanical frontiers of the contemporary cyber period have catered the need of the newly technically educated females. A few also have been represented in management posts as management personnel. As a matter of fact due to the increase in literacy of the women the women employment scenario is catching a momentum. Many authors have stated that women face variety of harassments and inhuman treatments Andippan 1979, Chakravorty 1975, Gulati 1979, Nanda 1975 Sinha and Ranade, 1975 Tilak 1980 while a few have written that women in general experience fewer obstacles in gaining promotions to day than ever before Mishra *et al.* 1986. Dissimilar wage for similar works has been the feature for female labour. All female labours get less wage than the male labour in most of the informal private sectors. In companies women managers and employees are expected to perform certain duties not mentioned in the work charts. Often due to the image and normative roles, and role conflicts may fail to meet the company objectives. Suneeta writes one woman in the group of men in a company is invariably overpowered and will fall back into her traditional subordinate roles if she is not prepared enough (1994).

Women face psychological and socio-cultural problems during movement from residence to work spot and back. Those who are introvert and almost voiceless and feel defenceless encounter the unacceptable norms. In a recent survey made by the author around 76 per cent of college girl students have opined that to almost all females specially young working and college going girls a few looks of the male folks are repelling and disturbing, a few of their actions are irritating and some responses are indicative of abnormal lust for animal behaviour towards sex. Women teacher have reported that women face problem but these can be reduced much if these not responded at all and further they stated that they need to re-examine and if necessary change their self image not only to avoid the awkward behaviour of the male towards the female but to generate assertive feature of their own. Self-concept is critical for personal achievement in which sex role identity is one of the most important attributes. The social conditioning acquired through the socialisation process in family, social and cultural values and the self-image of the female play vital role to become assertive.

For emancipation of women the changes in vital nexus between the social organisation, education and agitation have to be brought out strategically such that the women can acquire the skill of becoming assertive and have access to the resources and make themselves free from the male ideological bondages while manage the male to listen to them through informal negotiation to develop mutual understanding. The political will of the leaders, the awareness of the women on themselves, the induction of appropriate human value and human rights to all the male and female from the childhood as a part of socialisation and the participation of women in decision making processes for the distribution of resources would bring a perceptible change at least across the generations.

References

Andippan, P. 1986: Public Policy and discrimination in employment in India. *Indian Journal of Industrial Relations*. Vol. XIV, No. 3: 395–415.

Chakravorty, S. 1975: Farm women labour: waste and exploitation. *Social Change*. Vol. V, No. 1 and 2: 9–16.

Deghe, A. 1985: Womens employment in urban informal sector some critical issues. *Social Change*. Vol. 15, No. 2.

De Sauza, A, 1980: *Women in Contemporary India and South Asia*. Eds. Manohar Publication: New Delhi.

Guy, M.E., 1993: Three steps forward, two steps backward: The status of women's integration into Public management. *Public Administration Review*. Vol. 53, No. 4.

Majumder, Veena, 1983: The role of research in Women's development: A case study of the ICSSR programme on women studies. *Samaya Shakti*. Vol. 1, No. 1.

Majumdar, T., 1977: The urban poor and social change: A case study of squatter settlement in Delhi. *Social Action*. Vol. 27, No. 3.

Mishra, J.M., V.Vardhan, Kavita and V. Mishra, 1986: Woman managers in India and US: Analysis of attitudes, myths and skill. *Indian Management*, Vol. 25, No. 6: 25–29.

Nanda, A.K., 1975: Women in Industry. *Social Work Forum*. Vol. XIII, No. 3: 29 – 30.

Sinha, G.P. and S.N. Ranade, 1975: Women in developing economy II. Women construction workers Reports of two survey ICSSR. New Delhi: 79.

Seth, Mira 2001: *Women and Development: The Indian Experience*. New Delhi: Sage Publications.

Singh, Sunita, 1994: Development of women managers: myths and reality. *Management Spectrum*. Vol. 2, No. 1: 9–10.

Tilak, J.B.G., 1980: Education and labour market discrimination. *India Journal of Industrial Relations*. Vol. XVI, No. 1 : 95-114.

10

The Status of Women in Matrilineal Khasi Society

D. Sun

In most parts of North East area the women enjoy relatively better position compared to women in peninsular India mainly on account of their distinctive economic rights and roles. While the women in tribal societies of this region in general have better status, the Khasi, garo and sections of a few other tribes have more definite land rights and higher social position acquired by them through matrilineal and dual descent systems (Das 1982). Among the Khasi, Jaintia and Garo strong matrilineality provides the women rather higher positions with such definite rights as transmission of property in female line, transmission of name (title) of clan in female line and residence rule (matrilocality).

An attempt is made in this paper to portray the status of the Khasi women in the overall context of family and clan system, rules of marriage and Inheritance, particularly the property and ritual rights of the daughter, matrilocality, rules of succession, the women's role in management of the family and their economic role within the purview of the family and beyond as also their concern for social welfare.

The Khasi culture is one of the unique cultures of the world. Their culture is based on matriliny. It Is one of the few surviving matrilineal societies of the world.

The homeland of the Khasis is in the Khasi and Jaintia Hills of Meghalaya. It is bounded by Assam on the east and north and north-west and by Bangladesh on the south and south-west. The northern part of the Khasi territory Is known as Ri Bhoi which is formed of hillocks and flat lands amidst them. The central portion is known as Ri Lum which is dominated by ranges of hills and the southern region constitutes the Ri War region marked by steep slopes descending towards Sylhet area of Bangladesh.

We can divide the Khasis into the following territorial groups:

(i) The Kynriams of the central plateau of the Khasi Hills.

(ii) The Wars who Inhabit the War area in the south.

(iii) The Bhois who occupy the Bhoi area in the north, and

(iv) The Pnars of the Jaintia Hills who are also known as the Syntengs.

The origin of the Khasis Is a very vexed question and has been discussed at length by many others. Though they have inhabited their present abode for a considerable period, they believe that they are from elsewhere (Gurdon 1975 : 10). The Khasis are identified with the Mon-Khmer people of the Far-east mainly on the basis of language, megalithic culture and iron smelting. Modern linguistic studies have shown that there exist some important relations between the Khasi and the Mon-Khmer groups of languages. In the opinion of world renowned linguists like Pater Schmidt, Khasi in origin is Mon-Khmer of the Austric family (Austro-Asiatic). Close sisters of Khasi are probably the Palaung-Riang-wa dialects of Burma (Myanmar). The conformity of Khasi to Mon-Khmer is shown also in respect of gender, syntax, monosyllabic and also morphological construction (Barch 1964 : 4–5).

I

The Khasi tribe is composed of matri-clans, sub-clans and

family groups. All the matri-clans trace their origin to the ancient mother known as 'Ka lawbei Tynrai' who is the mother of the whole of 'shi kur' (clan). Next in order is 'Ka lawbei Tymen', the descendants of one great-grandmother of a sub-clan or 'Kpoh'. 'Ka lawbei Khynraw' is the ancestress, young grandmother of the family or 'ling'. It is invariably the case that the grandmother, her daughters and the ''daughter's children live together under one roof and the grandmother remains the head of the family. As the Khasis have the matrilineal social system the children identify themselves as members of mother's matri-clan and adopt the name of the mother's clan. The children born of a Khasi woman belong to the family of the mother. Every since the advent of the British periods when the first detailed documentation of Khasi matriliny was undertaken (vide Gurdon 1907), there has been no radical change In the matrilineal pattern of the Khasi and Jaintia people. Gurdon has provided a detailed description of the customs in vogue then in different Khasi territories and Doloi sips in the Jaintia Hills. He refers to the Khasi saying *long jaid na ka kynthei* (from the woman sprang the clan) which is fully relevant even today and which proves that the Khasi reckon descent from the mother only. At the same time the notion of *shi kpoh* (one womb, i.e., the Issue of one womb) further reaffirms the unilineality of the mother's descent line. While describing the situation further Gurdon has observed that a husband is looked upon merely as *U shong kha* a begetter. In some of the War Khasi villages, a newly married man Is spoken of by the bride's family as, *"u khun ki briew"* some one else's son. The fact that the husband Is a stranger in his wife's home, and it is certain that he can take no part in the rites and ceremonies of his wife's family, and that his ashes after death can find no place within the wife's family tomb, except in certain cases amongst the Syntengs.

Despite the fact that the Khasi and Jaintia strictly follow the norms and principles of matriliny in day to day social life people interact with each other in terms of their respective kinship statuses and rules. Thus, the two basic concepts of the Khasi society are those of '*Kur*' and '*Khait, kuris* the clan relationship and all kur members are descended from the same ancestral mother and *'Kha'* is that relationship which is generated through marriage' though of Kha relations only link two Individuals in the event of marriage. Hence, the kinship range of *Kha* is minimal.

II

Since time immemorial the Khasi women have been enjoying a considerably high status. The Khasi woman is newer looked down upon by the opposite sex but rather she is respected for who she is. In a Khasi family when a baby girl is born, it is proclaimed with pomp and show and she is not considered a burden to her parents or society. Just like a male child who has got the symbol of a bow and arrow placed in the altar when he is born, so also for the girl child a *'khoh'* (conical basket made of bamboo) and *"u star"* (a head strap made of cane) is kept in the altar signifying her birth, though this practise is no more in continuation in the urban areas[1].

The Khasi system of kin ship is based on clan exogamy and clans-people of a common ancestry could not intermarry. Intra-clan sexual relations-shlip is regarded as a mortal sin *'Ka sang'* and the persons who commit such a crime are excommunicated from the society. The members of the same *Kur* thus cannot inter-marry, no matter how far removed. The society places the demands of kinship as above the rule of the state and as at par with religions precepts (Miri in Mawrie, 1981 : 18). During the course of time, with the growth of members of a clan, dispersal took place and gradually such dispersed people acquired a sort of sub-clan identity, but they remained under one main clan. This identity is known as 'iateh kur'. For example, a person of the Sun clan cannot marry a person from the Lamare or Susngi clan. This is because they all share a common matrilineal

1. These symbols Indicate the Khasi people's intimate relation with forest environment. The bulk of the Khasi people indeed live in rural areas.

ancestry. Sch process of segmentation and also a critical analysis of Khasi matriliny has been provided by Das (1982,1989).

A non-Khasi woman who marries a Khasi man is not only accepted in the society but in due course she becomes the progenitress of a new clan. The *'Dkhar'* clans, several of which exist, originated in this way. Names of these clans start with the word *'Khar'* such a *Kharsohnoh, Kharkamni, Kharjana, Kharkongor* etc.

III

The Khasis have traditionally practised monogamy as the preferred form of marriage and the clan exogamy has been strictly observed from historical times till this day, despite adoption of the Christianity by a very large section among them. Marriage is a very important life cycle ritual for the Khasis. It provides not only a union between a man and a woman but it provides the base for establishing a new family. The Khasi girl is not necessarily kept out of the purview of the marriage negotiations. She is not forced into marriage alliance by her parents or relatives. Marriage is neither an agreement nor a contract but an understanding of the mind and thought of the two persons who agree to begin a family. This is one of the unique institutions of the Khasi society.

Neither the husband nor the wife in general parlance has a position lower than the other in their relationship but on account of matriliny certain special status and privileges are enjoyed by the woman. Their responsibility to their children Is shared jointly. The woman has her own status as a mother and the man, his own status as a father, and both of them know fully well that their family *'longing longsem'* can run smoothly based on their wisdom, knowledge, co-operation, love and understanding. With the adoption of the Christianity the notion of social equality of all individuals has been introduced. But indeed in the sphere of the domestic domain and even outside family it is matriliny and woman's specific clan status which counts. Somewhere indeed the, husband's identity and his status too is somewhat submerged within wife's matrilineally shaped family domain. All husbands however don't have to take up residence with his wife permanently in Mother-in law's residence. According to Gurdon also the Khasis are matrilineal, hence, it is not unusual for the husband to live in his mother-in-laws house after marriage. In other words, it is expected of him to stay there, but when one or two children are born, it is observed that such family moves out to establish a new house, where both husband and wife pool their earnings to support their newly made family (Gurdon 1975: 76). Amongst the Syntengs, however, and the people of Maoshai, the case is different, for with them the husband does not go and live in his mother-in-law's house, he only visits her there. If a Synteng house is visited, it Is unusual to find the husbands of any of the married daughters there, though the sons of the family may be seen in the house when they have returned from work. In the day time, the husbands of the married daughters are not there. The Syntengs, according to Gurdon seems to have more closely preserved the customs of the matriarchate than the Khasis, and the Syntengs claim that their *niam* or religious ceremonies are purer (Gurdon 1907 : 76).

After marriage, it is expected that a couple should be blessed with. children, for without a child, a woman can never become a mother. When a woman is pregnant, a ritual known as *Ka Tap Kpoh* (consecration of mother's womb) was carried out for the mother's health and safe delivery of the child. This practice may still presumably be in operation in rural areas of Khasi hills. There are several formalities involved in various life-cycle events such as birth, marriage, etc. The morning after a child is born, a ceremony known as *Jer khun* (naming ceremony) is performed. Three names are usually suggested and through divination to the Godhead and God of the clan, one name is selected for the child. Another ceremony is carried out after the naming ceremony known as *Ka Tap Lubri* (confirmation ceremony) to ensure the success in child's future life, as a human being.

The Khasi believe that when the child is in the mother's womb, it is in the protection of the Godhead, the Ancestress. For this reason, the stool passing out of the bowels of a new born is known as *ka eit iawbei* (Ancestress stool). When an infant parts the lips smilingly before attaining self-consciousness, the Khasi believe the child is in conversation with the Ancestress (*rkhie iawbei*). The scratch marks appearing on the belly of a mother after delivering a baby is known as *ka trud iawbei* (Ancestress scratch). The original hair of an infant not yet one year old is called *U Niuh iawbei* (Ancestress hair) and for this reason no knife, scissors or blade should touch the infant's head until it has crossed one year (Mawrie 1981 : 78).

It is the property rights of the Khasi women which provide them a unique social status. Traditionally, as per Khasi land tenure system, various categories of land are recognised such as *Ka ri Raj, Ka ri Syiem* which belong to the chief, and *Ka ri Lyngdoh*, belonging to the Priest. Then there are categories of land such as ri *Shnong*" (village land), *ki 'law kyntang* (sacred groves) and private lands. Under the private lands, two Important categories are *ri-kur* (clan land) and *ri-kynti* (family land). The manager of the clan land is Kni, maternal uncle of the youngest daughter.

The residence of the youngest daughter is called *Kaiing khadduh* in general parlance. However, since the ritual performances take place in the house of the youngest daughter, the said house is also referred to as *Kaiing seng*. Here, we notice the special Importance given to the traditional house of the mother where the socio-economic and ritual activities are performed and the same are distinctly recognised.

Thus, we may say that in the Khasi society all land acquired by inheritance must follow the Khasi law of inheritance, by which property descends from the mother to the youngest daughter and again from the latter to her youngest daughter. Ancestral landed property always transfer through the unilineal matriclan channel, making women the sole custodian of main source of the economy. Not only the youngest daughter but all her female siblings are fully protected economically in the tradition bound Khasi society. Hence, we see that daughters other than the youngest daughter are also entitled to maintenance from the property and produce of family lands.

As the mother's residential house *ling kmie* is also inherited by her youngest daughter, eventually she becomes its keeper and an organiser of family rites and rituals. The residential house may not be recognised strictly as her private or personal property, rather she lives in the house more in the capacity of a keeper since it is an ancegtral property. Though the residential house is inherited by the youngest daughter, she cannot dispose the same as also any properties or articles belonging to the family. For doing so, she will have to depend on the advice and also decisions from her maternal uncles, failing them her elder brothers who act as councellors. The totality of the ancestral property inherited by the youngest daughter is known as *'Ka nong tymmen'* . Properties and earnings which she may have accumulated in her lifetime is known as *'Ka nong khynraw'* (self-acquired property). This is solely hers and she can dispose, give or present the same to anyone she pleases in her lifetime. However, *'Ka nong khynraw'* does not include such land property which may be under the possession of the husband exclusively.

It is observed that in the traditional set up the social, economic and ritual relations of the Khasi society are all strongly woman-centric where the roles of the husband are extremely limited. Same is the case with male siblings though in the absence of the mother's brother, the role of brother is recognised, as discussed earlier.

V

In this section an attempt is made to describe the specific jural and ritual status of *Ka Khadduh* in the context of extra-family realms as also the situation arising due to her death. We shall also discuss the issue of adoption of an heiress for the family in order to avoid transmission of family property elsewhere. The *Ka Khadduh*, has important socio-economic, ritual and jural statuses in Khasi society traditionally. She takes the place of the mother, has a special duty in organising important religious rites and on such occasions her house forms a meeting place of her and her siblings' kith and kin. In accordance with her societal obligations she has to take care of her unmarried brothers and sisters. She also acts as a guardian to the parentless and homeless members of her family and when in need she provides shelter to them (Bareh 1964 : 9-10).

The duty and rights of the youngest daughter are still respected in both non-Christian and Christian segments of the Khasi society. In earlier times if a 'Khadduh' got converted to the Christianity, she was prohibited from participating in ritual rites and was also deprived of her rightful inheritance, but in contemporary times this is not the case any more. Even if a 'Khadduh' has embraced Christianity she can claim all her rights (Miri in Mawrie 1981 : 16-17).

As per the rule of matriliny in Khasi society if the youngest daughter dies, she is succeeded by the next youngest daughter, and so on. According to Kusum and Bakshi "if the youngest daughter is already married and have daughters of her own then the ancestral property goes to her own youngest daughter, howsoever low and if she be without any daughter her next elder sister inherits it and after her, the youngest daughter of that sister, howsoever low. Failing all daughters and their stock, the property reverts to the mother's family, i.e., to the mother's sister, and so on" (1982 : 97).

When the need arises the Khasi even today resort to adoption of a girl from same matri-clan, as far as possible. To quote Gurdon. "If in a Khasi and Synteng family, all female members have died out, the male members of the family are allowed to call a girl from some other family of the same *jaid* (meaning clan) to act as *ka rapping*, and to perform the family religious ceremonies. The female so introduced takes the place as *ka khun khadduh*, and becomes the head of the house (ka training). The adoption of a female obviates the family dying out (*iap duh*) which to a Khasi is a very serious matter. In the case of a family being *iap duh* (extinct/dying out) the family property, according to Khasi custom, passes to the Syiem. Therefore, it is to the interest of the members of families to adopt a female when such necessity arises" (1907 : 85-86).

VI

The Khasi society being matrilineal, the property is inherited by the womenfolk. They are however, not entitled to succeed to the offices of Chieftains, but when the situations arise and when there is scarcity of male successors, women have been allowed to succeed to the Offices of Chieftainship. There are several instances when, in the past, many female Syiems had taken over the duty of administration. Also, traditionally, only in the presence of male successors, that the Syiem mothers nominated a Syiem to succeed to his deceased predecessor. In other words, the nobles had to consult senior Syiem mothers to fill up a vacant Office of Syiemship (Bareh 1964 :40).

The ancestral residence of the Khasi Syiem is called ling-*Sad* and its keeper is Ka Syiem-Sad. She is considered as the custodian of religious rites which belong to her family and the Syiemship. With the assistance of the male priests, she performs all sacredotal duties. Hence the Khasi political system has a direct reference to religion. Their state craft has a strong religious bias. The *Syiem-Sad* is either the mother or the senior aunt or a sister of the ruling Syiem. *'Sad'* refers to everything that concerns the state from religion to daily activities. In this close Interdependence of religion and state (*Niam* and *Hima*) with the *Syiem-Sad* as the protector of both, the term '*U Syiem U Kmie* meaning 'King and Mother' has come into vogue (Mathur

1979 : 79-80). It is important to note that a Syiem ruler conducts his official duties from *Ka ling-Sad* though he lives apart at his wife's residence. The *ling-Sad* is considered a religious house of the State besides serving as an office, court and meeting place of official councils.

Syiem-Sads are title holders of crown lands (Ri-Syiem) and a Syiem-Sad is "a spiritual head of the State who delegates the ruling powers to a Syiem ruler", either her maternal uncle, brother or son.

The Khasis being a matrilineal society, kingship does not pass from father to son, as is generally carried out in rest of India. A nephew or grand-nephew succeeds to his maternal or grand-maternal uncle who held office during his lifetime. The Syiem-ruler is assisted by another prince called *U Syiem Khynnah* (junior prince) elected from the Syiem's family. Both male and female Syiem (Syiem-Sad) were elected and were duly confirmed at investiture ceremonies (Bareh 1964 : 40-42).

Much of political relevance of the Syiemship may have diminished after the advent of the wider democratic state, but many social, cultural, religious and economic functions associated with the Syiem have survived, till today. Mathur (1979) has observed that "the prolonged contact of the Khasi people with Christianity and western civilization has not undermined the traditional religion, which is the core of the Khasi culture and the age-old political institutions. The Syiems still wield great influence. The potent Syiem leadership finds full expression in the Nongkrem festival in which the community dance is an important part. It is a festival for invoking the blessings of the ancestress clans, the founders of the 'Khasi state' and other respected ancestors. This festival has helped to forge the ties of solidarity among different sub-tribes and the Khasi, both non-Christian and Christian are keen on preserving the traditional political institutions associated with religious practices".

VII

An important feature of the Khasi society is that the women invariably tend to remain independent economically. Though a woman enjoys good social status and economic rights on account of inbuilt security provided by the matriliny but she is always conscious and eager to contribute towards family income even when she is not able to derive much sustenance from ancestral property. As a result, the women have increasingly engaged themselves in many economic activities including service, professions, business and trade. There are many women who engaged in selling of fish and vegetables in the market place (*lewduh*). Studies of Marak and Das (1972) show that Khasi males generally seek employment in various government offices. The numerical dominance of women in trade is in contrast to what we usually see in other tribal and non-tribal areas in India and elsewhere.'

In the market place (in Bara Bazar of Shillong) there are many small hotels and eating places where traditional Khasi food items are available in plenty. There are Jadoh (Rice-meat, a Khasi speciality) stalls or restaurants where only Khasi food specialisties are served to the customers. Alongwith the 'Jadoh' other dishes such as dohkhlieh (beef or pork mixed with onions, ginger and salt), tungrymbai (made from beans), etc., are also served. These stalls too are exclusively run by the women folk mainly the Pnars of Jaintia Hills.

Majority of the women traders who do business in Shillong are from different areas outside Shillong and who came to the city for a better economic prospect. A majority of them were agriculturists before (Sen, Saha, Mukherjee 1982). There are however, a large number of women who have not engaged themselves in trading work particularly in rural areas and they work as cultivators and agricultural labourers in the fields where they practise both shifting and wet paddy cultivation. They also grow potato, orange, pineapple, betel-nut and betel-leaf.

The role of Muslim Khasi women in the economy of the urban areas is worth mentioning. Mathur has studied the social and economic life of the Muslim Khasi women. The Muslim-Khasi women work as confectioners, bakers and petty traders. They assist their husbands in their petty trade and business (Mathur 1979 : 50).

From an earlier stage, the enlightened Khasi women were concerned about the development of their society. Hence, to help in rooting out the old habits they started forming associations. One prominent association has been that of the 'Synjuk Kynthei ('Women's' association). Though it is a non-religious association, but both the Christian and non-Christian women participate in it. Their main aim is to improve the social and cultural life of the members of the Khasi society. Their programme included moving from house to house mainly in the rural areas and imparting the knowledge about knitting, stitching, family planning, healthy ways of living, maternity, etc. This association was patronised by the Central Social Welfare Board. The Christian Missionaries also lend them a hand in their activities. This association has opened one Rural Welfare Centre in Mylliem Syiemship, where the members give training to the village women and their children. It has also trained many Khasi women on nursing and *dhai* work.

The 'Seng Pynduh Kiad' (Liquor Prohibition Association) is another women's association whose aim is to remove Alcoholism from the Khasi and Jaintia Hills. Its main office is in Shillong town. The members very often go to the villages and discuss with the villagers about the bad effects of Alcoholic drinks. According to the members of the 'Seng Pynduh Kiad' they are getting much support from the villagers rather than the urban areas (Marak and Das, 1973). In Mawdat-baki, a locality of Mawlai (Shillong), the women have had an associations under the name of the 'Seng Kyrthei' which has made forceful appeals to the public at large about the ill-effects of liquor and had worked with zeal for about five from 1982—88 years to eradicate the selling of liquor in that locality as liquor at that time was illegally sold in many Khasi homes, and which provided a means of livelihood. Every night the members of the Association will raid the houses which were suspected of selling liquor, and with the help of youths throw the gallons of liquor into the streets. This act of the Seng Kynthei was praised by one and all and after the 5 years long movement they succeeded in their mission and uptodate, the illegal selling of liquor is not done in that area (Personal communication, Mrs. W. Sun).

VIII

The tribal women in NE India enjoy a relatively better position compared to women of the rest of India mainly on account of their hereditary land rights and roles acquired through matrilineal and dual descent based social systems. Even in those societies where patriliny is the norm of society the women have traditionally enjoyed greater freedom, and statuswise their existence and their roles are of equal value vis-a-vis those of the male folk. Among the tribes of NE India, the Khasi including Jaintia, the Garo, the Dimasa, Semsa, Lalung, Hajong and Koch recognise the specific rights of the women as these tribes represent extreme matriliny and moderate matriliny respectively. Among these tribes it is the Khasi and the Garo who pursue rigid forms of matriliny compared to the tribes such as the Dimasa, Semsa, Lalung, Hajong and Koch.

Among the Dimasa, who follow the dual descent system, a woman Inherits property from her mother and a son inherits property from his father. Ritually, also the Dimasa women are given equal status as the men. Among the Semsa, the concept of *patrikin* and *matrikin* have been extended upto patriclan (*sengfong*) and matriclan (*jaddi*). The property owned by women are transmitted through female line only (Danda 1984, Das 1997).

Among the Lalung (Das 1982) we find the co-existence of matrilineal and patrilineal inheritance patterns. Among them the clans are matrilineal but the rules of patriliny now govern the general mode of transmission of property. The Hajong who live in the Garo Hills formerly had exogamous matrilineal clans. The Koch, whose one segment lives in Maghalaya, are basically organised on the basis of matrilineal clans (*nikini*) but due to their close cultural interaction with the plains people, have changed their traditional inheritance rule and hence the women are not entitled to enjoy landrights any more (Das 1982).

The women in Khasi society derive their economic rights through matriliny. The Khasi and the Garo according to Das resemble similarity in basic succession-inheritance, rules of mother-daughter and mother's brother-sister's son. In fact, the property is owned by the women but the management falls in the hands of the men. The property group of the Khasi is formed by a descent group at a shallow generation depth while that of the Garo is maintained by the co-operation of the two local lines, each of which represents a localised lineage group. Hence, the Garo descent group tends to be weak. Turning to descent group formation, while among the Garo, the localised lineage is expressed in terms of the village whose land bears the name of localised lineages; among the Khasi, on the other hand the lineage is found only on a household scale, within the unit of iing" (1982). Among the Garo the heiress (*Nokna*) to the property is daughter who is selected by a group of male relations in the context of the *Mahari*, a socio-territorial unit. In order to maintain the continuity with the *Mahari*, the nephew is incorporated as son-in-law. It is this process of incorporation of the nephew in Garo system which makes it a less rigid form of matriliny compared with the Khasi (Das 1997).

Traditionally, the Khasi society had provided no scope for the women to participate in the political arena, outside the family domain. The Khasi society recognised the male members as the head of the state and the elders for the *Durbar* (council) were recruited from amongst the male members, though there were a few exceptions to this rule. Following traditional arrangements, presumably the women were generally kept out of the purview of political and administrative domain. The fact remains that in popular parlance also quite a few male-centric notions have been in vogue which may have discouraged the women to enter Into the political field. One such common notion is that *'u rangbah Khlem u tmain, ymlah ban shong durbar'* (a man without a moustache cannot attend a Durbar).

Conclusion

Today there is a great spurt in educational attainment among the Khasi women and they have also gone for professional courses and technical expertise. This has facilitated the women-folk to get involved in service-profession sector in a big way, generally outside the state, unlike in the past when they were confined to family level, petty trade and shopkeeping. This has however provided only partial empowerment to the women folk in economlc sphere. This author is of the view that the women-centric value system derived from matriliny has essentially prompted the Khasi people to educate and build up women to gain greater economic independence. It may however be added here that the tradition of imparting education to girls has a long tradition which goes back to the early cononial period when the educational activities of missionaries were launched in the Khasi hills. Among the Khasi while on the one hand the matriliny continues to provide the women higher economic status through transmission of property in female line, transmission of clan name in female line and matrilocal residence, at the same time through formal education and participation in service and professional sectors in modern times, unprecedented economic independence is now enjoyed by the Khasi women, but it has not resulted in providing greater empowerment to the Khasi women particularly in terms of their participation in politico—democratic fields and in the process of decision-making.

References

Bareh, H. 1964: *Khashi Democracy,* Shillong: Ri Khasi Press.

Danda, Dipali, G., 1984: A note on the Semsa - A section of the Dimsa. *In the Tribes of North East India*, Sebastian Karotemprel (Ed.) Calcutta: Firma KLM Private Ltd.

Das, N.K., 1982: Review of the works on social structure of some matrilineal tribes of North East India and observation thereon. *Indian Anthrop. Soc.* 17(3): 199-214.

Das, N.K., 1989: *Ethnic Identity, Ethnicity and Social Stratification in North East India*, New Delhi: Inter-India Publications.

Das, N.K., 1997: Status and land rights of the tribal women in North East India; in *Contemporary Society: Trilal Studies*. George, P. and D.K. Behera (Eds.) Vol. I, pp. 197–203.

Gurdon, P.R.T., 1975: *The Khashi.* Delhi: Cosmo Publication.

Mathur, P.R.G., 1997: *The Khasis of Meghalaya*. New Delhi: Cosmo Publication.

Mawrie H.O., 1981: *The Khasi Milieu*. New Delhi. Concept Publishing Company.

Marak, S.A. and Das, M.M. 1973: A few aspects of the Khasis of Shillong. *Bulletin of the Anthropological Survey of India*. Vol. XXII (1–2): 86–175.

Nianglang, P.S., 1999: The marriage ceremony of the Non gtrais. *Journal of the North East India Council for Social Science Research*. Vol., 23 (2): 14-17.

Sen, Jyoti, N. Saha and S.U. Mukherjee, 1982: Role of Women in Tribal Economy. In *Economics of the Tribes and their Transformation*. Eds. K.S. Singh: pp. 95–103.

11

The Status of the Ladiya Women

Dipak K. Adok

Introduction

History informs us that once upon a time a matrilineal form of society characterized the societies of the world. Women, in such society enjoyed many privileges—autonomy, equality and even superiority, dignity, property rights, etc. Today, there are only a few remnants of this form of society in the world, and the patrilineal form dominates the world—a society in which privileges are the property of men, and women are generally regarded as inferior (Chaurasia, 1994).

In general, the attitude of the males towards the females that persists in the traditional garb is shaped by a notion of superiority which has rather been to imposing and repressing. History tells that the women have, most of the time, suffered at the hands of the men. Elements of incompetence, incapability, lack of understanding, etc. have often been regarded as attributes of the women. Though a good deal of studies on the position of women has been made in different parts of our country, such studies are still seant in central India. In the present study the status of the women has been assessed in various walks of life among the Ladiya of Pathariya jat village of Sagar district, Madhya Pradesh.

The People

For the sake of present study the Ladiya residing in Pathariya Jat village of Sagar district, Madhya Pradesh have been taken into consideration. The Ladiya is a sub-group of the Chamar Scheduled Castes community of Madhya Pradesh. They are landless people with dependence on labour in urban area. Their men are mainly engaged as daily labourer (30.21 per cent), bidi worker (26.56 per cent) and skilled worker (25 per cent), whereas most of the women are engaged in bidi making occupation (75.53 per cent). However, a good number of them are also housewives (Adak and Gharami 1999)

Field Method

An exhaustive schedule was prepared for data collection. This schedule was filled in case of 180 informants of the village. To get the women's perspective the filling of 180 schedules was restricted to the women's informants of the village. However, as certain notion of avoidance prevails, it was not possible to isolate the womenfolk from menfolk during field work as the observer is a male anthropologist.

Status of the Women

In this study a few domains of social life such as preference of male sex, attitude to male/female in family, adoption, inheritance, succession, marriage and divorce only are viewed for determining the position of the Ladiya women. The Ladiya society being a patrilineal Hindu society follows the rules and customs as applicable to Hindu caste groups elsewhere, hence the preference for the males, who have the inbuilt, predetermined superior ritual and legal status vis-a-vis the females.

Preference of Male Sex

As described above the predominance and superiority of the male sex exists in the Ladiya society. Only 2.82 per cent of the respondents expressed their attitude in favour of the females in family. The reasons behind the preferential attitudes towards the males as derived from the data are as follows:

(1) That the male member stays with the parents and serves them in old age, whereas the daughter leaves the parental house after she gets married;

(2) That the boy is more useful in a family as he has greater physical fitness to earn more;

(3) That only the male members has the privilege of performing last rites in the event of parents death, and

(4) That the male can be sent to work outside, but a female cannot.

A small number of women respondents who spoke in favour of female, stated that the females should also "enjoy equal right with men and they deserve it too". These view are expressed by those women who are exposed to education and urban areas.

Attitude to Male/Female in Family

It is found that the overwhelming majority of the Ladiya expressed their view about the superior position of the male over female. The reasons behind this are:

(1) That the male is head of the family while the female is subordinate to him; and

(2) That the male is more capable of decision-making in regard to family affairs and also in the affairs outside the household.

Adoption

In the Ladiya society the childless couples go for adoption of male or female child due to various compulsions. The preference is most often in favour of the male child. In general a child of the close relative of the husband is adopted. The reasons behind the adoption are;

(1) that in old age the adopted son looks after the parents, whereas the adopted daughter gets married and leaves parental place; and

(2) that only the son inherits the parental property.

Inheritance

Among the Ladiya the items of property which are subjected to inheritance include land, house and livestock. The majority of them subscribed the view that the women are deprived of any claim over the property. It is indeed the custom of the Ladiya people to give the sole inheritance right to menfolk. Nearly 70.36 per cent of the respondents stated that the females do not inherit any property. The women inherit property only when no male heir is available.

Succession

Pattern of succession among the Ladiya follows the inheritance pattern prevalent in society which determines the relative positions of the members in society. So the rule of patriliny which governs the Ladiya social structure ensures the headship of the son in the family after the death of the father.

Marriage

Traditionally the Ladiya preferred marriage of girls at an early age. There is certain change noted in this respect. However, there is no liberty enjoyed by the girls in mate selection in case of marriages which are arranged ones. The parents themselves select the mate. The orthodox character of local caste system is responsible for this situation whereby the women are largely denied the right to choose the mate. In regard to the form of marriage the Ladiya are mainly monogamous.

Divorce

Cases of divorce and simple separation are not uncommon. Men have often separated wives for simple reasons. There are also cases when women have sought divorce, on account of husband's extravagency and excessive drunkenness. The occurrence of divorce has its root in oppressive male oriented social, economic and biological parameters shaping social life.

A positive dimension of changing position of Ladiya women

is reflected in a few cases when the matter of separation has been brought before the court by the parents of the deserted women. In such cases compensation and redressal is claimed and recovered from the male members.

It is observed that the traditional socio-cultural norms and practices of the Ladiya has resulted in severe discrimination and deprivation of the womenfolk. The responses collected highlight that the traditional social system maintains its rigidity and accords a very low status to the women. The rural Ladiya are still in the grip of traditional norms and practices where the females are dominated by the males. The deprivations and denials of women are deep-rooted in the social structure of the Ladiya. In this backdrop some proposals for the upliftment of the Ladiya women need to be made. What is also required is a change of attitude on part of menfolk of the Ladiya which may be possible by making them educated and better employed.

References

Adak, D.K. and A.K. Gharami, 2001: A study on the population composition of the Ladiya of Sagar District, Madhya Pradesh. *South Asian Anthropolozist*, 1 (2): 83—89, New Series.

Chaurasia, A., 1994: Dimensions of Status of Women in Developing Countries. *The Journal of Family Welfare*, 40(3): 42–50.

12

Status of Women in Rural Society with Special Reference to Polyandry of Garhwal Himalaya

Alok Chantia

The Indian peninsula contains a total of 437 tribal groups, out of which 40 are polyandrous. They can be classified as 28 being fraternal polyandrous, 5 are non-fraternal polyandrous, 7 are mixture polyandrous. But polyandry in the Himalayan region of Garhwal is well-known to every-one. It is also a matter of discussion that most tribal groups are engaged in agriculture. So tribals should be included in the rural society. Due to heavy population, scarcity of food, unemployment, tribalization has increased. In 1967, the government declared Khasa as a tribe in the light of their queer characteristic polyandry. After seeing the parameter—polyandry, in deciding a group as a tribe, the people of an adjacent area of Khasa tribe declared themselves, a tribe with a strange name *Jaunsar Bawar*. While Dr. Majumdar described only one tribe in Garhwal Himalaya, (i.e., Khasa), who engaged, in polyandry. So in my paper, I will discuss the use of the term *Jaunsar Bawar*,

'Alok Chantia, Lecturer (Anthropology), Jai Narayan P.G. College, Lucknow.
Mailing Address : Alok Chantia, 124, Shekheiya Pura, Bahraich - 271801.

which has brought about a change in the status of woman of this region.

Jaunsar Bawar lies in the Chakrata tehsil of district Dehradun, Jaunpur lies in the Dhanaulti tehsil of Tehri district and Rawain in the Purola and Barkot tehsil of Uttarkashi district. Lying adjacent to each other, these tracts constitute a geographi-cultural chunk of polyandry in the Garhwal Himalaya in Uttaranchal. They lie in a inaccessible mountainous terrain, the topographical rigours of which make life exacting, and as assumed in the academics of polyandry fuinctional.

Here it is notable that the inhabitants of Jaunsar Bawar are a Schedule Tribe, but not those of Rawain Jaunpur though like the former, they also practice polyandry and are structured in a similar caste-stratification.

In Chakrata tehsil of Dehradun, the local caste structure is discernible into three stratification levels, i.e., the upper (land owning castes—the Rajputs and the Brahmins), the middle (artisan castes—the Nath, the Bajgi, the Mistri and the Lohar), and the lower (unclean castes—the Kolta, the Chamar and the Dom). Among these, the castes of the upper and the lower levels are more numerous than those of the middle level. They also show a higher incidence of polyandry. Because of these changes, this correlation between caste-structure and polyandry is now clianging, though not evenly.

Jaunsar Bawar claims their association with the Pandavas. Is it true? Do women normally union with several husbands? In the *Mahabharat*, Draupadi is *bahubhartrika*, but not Subhadra, the second wife of Arjuna. Other wives whom the Pandava brothers individually, like Hidimba (Bhim's wife), were also not shared. Only Draupadi was shared by common consent.

The inhabitants of these tracts claim spiritual and mythical affinity with the Pandava of the *Mahabharata*. The Pandava dance and the worship of Draupadi in certain areas in the biannual ritual celebration (at the time of each harvest) evidently symbolize this relationship. But here, unlike Draupadi, the wife is not won in a competition of archery. Nor has she the right to *swayamvar* as such. She is rather purchased and shared as a wife.

A comparison of the similarities and variations in the practices of polyandry in the Rawain Jaumpur and Jaunsar Bawar throws much light on the whys of polyandry, its dynamics and a woman's place in it. Jaunsar Bawar show a higher incidence (48.3 per cent) of polyandry than the Rawain Jaunpur (30.56 per cent).

Disparity of the sexes is wider in Jaunsar Bawar, here being 820 females for 1000 males, as against 996.56 females for 1000 males in the Rawain Jaunpur. The correlation between wider disparity of sexes and higher incidence of polyandry is obvious, though not casual. Showing a wider disparity of sexes, the castes of the middle level don't register a corresponding higher incidence of polyandry. In Rawain Jaunpur, two brothers generally born one after another, generally share one, two or three wives. In Jaunsar Bawar, two to five brothers have been found sharing one to four wives.

Both in Jaunsar Bawar and the Rawain Jaunpur, a woman thas to compensate her husband, if she forces the dissolution of marriage. Even a widow has to acquire freedom to remarry, by compensating her deceased husbaind's family-in certain cases, even her son. In Jaunsar Bawar, she compensates for the expenses incurred on marrying her and in Rawain Jaunpur for the price paid for her. Sometimes, expenses incurred on the wife's maintenance and treatment may also be demanded and added to the compensation charged. Depending on the negotiations and consequent agreement, interest on the amount of bride price paid and/or on the expenses incurred in marriage may also be charged.

In all these tracts, a daughter is viewed as an asset of her father, a wife of her husband and a widowed woman of her son and the deceased husband's family. In the exigencies of life, to look to her father, brother and brother's son is a woman's privilege, which is honoured as her right. The tradition allows a woman the right to remarry, but the traditional liability to compensate the husbands, she divorces (*choot ka paisa dena*) also constraints this right. She plays a vigorous role in the local household and agricultural economy. Yet she is viewed as impure and, like an untouchable is denied temple entry.

The worldwide view about woman is a more meaningful social reality relating to woman in polyandry. Woman is a dependable source of labour needed for agriculture and household work. She is needed to procreate sons, for whom there is definite preference. She is a possession, an asset. As a daughter, she is to be given in marriage for a price. As wife she can be fraternally shared like land, if brothers sharing her agree to do so. This also explains sexual sharing of a set of wives by a set of brothers, though wives may be brought and kept in the individual names of the brothers.

Why polyandry? The question is not purely academic, when examined in the perspective of *dam vivah* and woman's place in it and in polyandry. The directive principles of Indian Constitution relating to uniform civil code and the amelioration of the weaker sections (to which women belong) lead to this question as its political undertones.

It is said "polyandry is a functional consequence of disparity of sexes, scarcity of land, difficult mountainous terrain, labour, intensive agriculture, coupled with sheep and goat rearing and domestication of cattle. This setting necessitates joint living at the level of household, of which sharing of wife is the most outstanding feature. The growing politics of being polyandrous tribal is a consequence of that, on the basis of polyandry and the claim of not practicing Hinduism and untouchability. The elite of Jaunsar Bawar could wrest for the region, the political status of Scheduled Tribe under an irrelevant fragile title, the

Jaunsari tribe—and the advantages of protective discrimination flowing there from (Bhoria 1975). This smacks of a muffled political compromise on the woman's status as *bahubhartrika*.

However, this political move has been challenged since then, the status of a Scheduled Tribe for all the Jaunsari, it is pointed out, promotes the interest of the elitist castes (the Brahmin and the Rajput) at the cost of those of the middle and the lower strata, the have-nots. Since then, a bill has also been pending to exclude the Brahmin and the Rajput from the status of Scheduled Tribe. To retain the status of Schedule Tribe, the elite in Jaunsar Bawar lift arguments from the writing of academicians. They argue that the custom of polyandry or making woman *bahubhartrika* is functional to the social economy. It need not be disturbed, meaning thereby that their status as a Scheduled Tribe should be secured. Following the Jaunsaris, the inhabitants of Rawain Jaunpur have also been demanding and politically lobbying for the status of Scheduled Tribe.

In this politics, a woman's position as *bahubhartrika* and problems associated there with get relegated to the background: It is tending to reinforce polyandry as a vested elitist interest. The crumbling faeade of polyandry has tended to become a sort of political lever to retain or attain the status of Scheduled Tribe.

In the light of status of woman of the Garhwal Himalaya in a polyandrous society, women suffered due to the judgement of Supreme Court. In case of Dr. Surajmani Vs. Durgacharan 2001 (42) ALR-847, in which the honorable judge said, "Hindu Marriage Act 1955 covers whole India, but those groups are excluded who do their marriage with special custom". In this regard polyandry cannot be challenged. So the whole geographical chunk of Garhwal Himalaya for polyandry haas been protected by court. But this judgement makes worse the position of those women who are not tribal but practicing polyandry (the Brahmin and the Rajput).

This is a real picture of rural woman in the Garhwal Himalaya, who are the victim of customs, politics and the judiciary.

References

Bhatt, G.S. 1992: *Women in Polyandry in Rawain and Jaunpur. Jaipur, Rawat Publications.*

Bhoria, K.S., 1975: The case of Jaunsarim as a Scheduled Tribe. *Journal of Lal Bahadur* Shastri National Academy of Administration, XX (2).

Bierreman, G.G., 1963: *Hindus of the Himalayas*. Bombay, Oxford.

Majumdar, D.N., 1944: *The Fortunes of Primitive Tribes*. Lucknows, Universal Publishers.

13

Women Participation in Village Panchayat

Kalpana Saini

Biologically, the status of women is based on sex-dichotomy. But for all types of activities it is not established with certainty that what is biological and what is cultural in sex differentiation. It is true that certain physiological functions are sex-linked. women possess the basic reproductive role which is biologically fixed. This is the reason that every society assigns different roles to male and females and expects from them to behave differently. The division of labour on the basis of sex is found to be present in all societies whether they are modern societies or primitive and according to the role their status is determined.

India is a big country and the status of women is not uniform in all the rural areas of the country. Variations can be seen from place to place and even within the same population groups living in different ecological cultural settings. Factors like, rules of residence, descent, inheritance, marriage, divorce and degree of acculturation, urbanization, modernization and many such factors contribute to this variation. Though the Constitution of India provides equality of status to Indian women with men but whether they have attended the equality in real sense. As we know, there always exists a gap between theory and practice. It is not merely equality under law that determines the status of women in a society but traditions and customs are more powerful than law in determining women's position within a social structure.

The declaration of International Women's Year by United Nations during 1975 and subsequently with the explosion of mass media, women all over world have started redefining their position and thrown challanges to the age-old male-dominated system of the society. Now the women are awken and they are not only satisfied with the developmental benefits often given to them in the form of concession or compassion but they want equal share in the total national resources. They want equal status and equal power in the society. But this is limited to the modern societies only. In rural societies, women's are generally a depressed group. They are still continuing to play a more active role as a bread earner of the family. Male dominence is a consequence of their exclusive role in the extra-domestic sphere, which fetches their status and freedom to act independently. They are deprived of educational, occupational, social, religious and political rights.

Conscious of the emergence of the new awakening in women, governments all over the world have started giving share to the women in the power structure of society. Over the years the Government of India has also been putting efforts to evaluate the social status of women and has announced many policies for their upliftment like, reservations in education, jobs and also in political front. quota have been fixed for the women in different offices of *panchayat* and also in Municipal bodies.

In Madhya Pradesh, the seats for women are reserved for the offices of *Panchas* and *Sarpanchas* for the *Panchayats* of the villages. In recently concluded *panchayat* elections in the state many women have been returned and occupied different positions in many officies in the village *panchayat* according to their quota. No doubt, this has given a rank to the women, which was earlier a dream to them but as I previously said that there always exists a gap between theory and practice.

Let us examine, whether this quota based Panchayati Raj system has brought any conspicuous change in the status of women? Theoretically, there are three indicators by which one can assess the change of status.

They are:

(1) Interactional position in the society,

(2) Participation in community, and

(3) Decision making.

On the basis of these three indicators we can assess whether the quota based *Panchayati* system have brough any change in the status of women in rural societies.

Let us see the present interactional position of women in society. It is true that by becoming Pancha and Sarpancha their rank is elevated but it fails to bring any change in their interaction in social structure. She continues to perform the traditional role in the family-setup. She is still busy with hearth and kitchen in the family. Their position with their husband remains almost unaffected. The domination of husband in the family is still prevalent. The male members of the family take decisions in all matters concerning the kins. The behavioural pattern in kinshi structure also remains same. The male members of the clan continue to maintain their hold over caste Panchayat. It is seen that by merely obtaining a high status as a Pancha or a Sarpancha in the village, the rural womens are not enjoying the similar status like many other counterparts as a beautiful drawing room show piece in advanced societies. This clearly indicate that the position of women in Panchayat does not appear to have effected change in the interactional position of the women.

Now the question comes that by holding a position of Pancha or a Sarpancha in the village panchayat do the villagers or the persons of her own caste treat the women in a different manner?

We know well that in Indian society the area of community

participation for an Indian women is fixed. According to the traditions and customs the Indian women can participate only in a few community activities. In village culture their are few barriers to which the Indian women is bound to follow. A Indian women cannot go alone to attend a community meeting or even if she goes alone she cannot stayes after sunset. Talking with other males of the village or even with some of the family relatives is not a common practice in most of the Indian villages. As soon as a women becomes Pancha or a Sarpancha the area of her community participation becomes broad. As a Sarpancha she has to visit many times to the collector's office or to the office of a Tahasildar and very frequently to the Block Office regarding the village work and in many cases these offices are far away from her village. During her visit to these offices she has to meet number of male persons and number of times she has to stay there after sunset too. But according to the village norms she cannot do all this and this restrict her community participation. If a women dares to go against the village norms for the sake of the walfare activities of the village, she becomes the talk of the village, this is more when the women happens to be young. Looking to the norms of the village generally, the husband do not permit her wife to do so. In such conditions a women is often escorted by her husband or accompanied with her near relative. When a women is accompanied by her husband, her community participation depends on the wishes of her husband or some other male person who accompanied her. In case, when her husband or the other family members are not free and they are unable to take her to the block office or Collectorate, she has no other choice but to cancel her important meeting. These type of restrictions are bound to cause serious damage in the development of the village.

III

In Indian social structure, normally the decision making power rests with the male members of the family. Though in advanced societies this norm is changed but in rural societies it is still prevalent. Normally in the villages the decision making power either rests with the father or with the husband or even in some cases with the son also. This clearly indicates that the traditional collectiveness still maintain the hold over rural women. But in a changed scenario, after becoming Pancha or Sarpancha she has to take Secisions in the village panchayat and here a women goes under tremendous pressure in passing orders and making decisions because she was never been involved in decision making in the past. It is also seen that male persons of the Panchayat generally do not accept her decisions seriously. In our country the literacy rate of the females are poor. Most of the female Panche and Sarpanchas are illiterate. They neither read nor write. The decisions taken by them are generally written by the other male Panchayat members. So it is always questionable whether the decisions taken by them are written correctly or not. This clearly show that the involvement of women Sarpancha in decision making is not very encouraging and it is only for the name sake.

A few weeks ago, I visited a rural village near to our town in connection with some data collection and happend to have a chance to meet a lady who is Sarpancha of that village. She is 52 years of age and have nine children. Her youngest son is of 5 years of age. She is a illiterate lady and she cannot read or write but she can write her name only, which she has learned from her husband after holding the office of Sarpancha in a village Panchayat. I had a talk with her and also with some village people about the functioning of the village panchayat. The answers which I received from them are quite surprising. The women Sarpancha of that village hardly attend meetings of the Panchayat. On her behalf the meetings were attended by her husband. Her husband brings official documents or files to her home and there she put her signature on them. Quite interestingly, it all happens in the presence of government officers and they overlook it. The biggest joke is that a women Sarpancha who is supposed to give direction to the whole village is herself being given direction by her husband. Precisely, this is the condition of the other villages of our country also, where a women Is a Pancha or a Sarpancha on the basis of quota fixed for them.

Looking to the above facts, it can be said that a women hold-ing an office in the quota based panchayat system does not bring a substantial change in her status. The sad part of the story is that the government of today has provided all powers and a high position to a women in village Panchayat but because of lack of awareness she is fully deprived from them. If the government is really serious in enhancing the status of women, then efforts should be made first to literate them and make them aware about their status and role in the society. This can only be done by providing equal opportunities for education, condition of self-reliance, economic independency and equal occupational opportunities for men and women. Equal occupational opportunities for men and women will definitely call males to participate in domestic affairs as well like females.

14

Relative Political Status of Rural Women (A Case Study from Eastern Rural Uttar Pradesh)

A.R.N. Srivastava • Sangeeta Sinha

The Background

There are probably as many definitions of 'status' as there are researchers in the field interested in the topic. 'Relative status of sexes' to some means how much importance a society confers on women versus men. To others it means how much power and authority women or men have relative to each other. And to still others, it means what sort of right women and men possess and what they want to do. It has become an important issue to sociologists and anthropologists to think about why do women have few right and little influence in some societies but more of each in other societies? Simply put it, why is there gender variation?

In his illumienating cross cultural study Whyte (1978) could not arrive at any definite conclusions. He rated 52 different items used in defining the relative status of the sexes. Some of these

---

*Prof. A.R.N. Srivastava is in anthropology at University of Allahabad and Dr. Sangeeta Sinha is Lecturer in Sociology at Government P.G.College Chakia (Chandauli District).

items included inheritance of property by sex or gods and goddesses, warfare, political decision, subsistence, among others. Whyte found very few items are related; therefore, he concluded one cannot talk about status as a single concept.

It would seem more appropriate to talk about the relative status of women in different sphere of life (Whyte: 1978; 95 – 120)

The Area and the People

In post-independence era Uttar Pradesh has emerged as a laboratory for foraging new tools and concepts in sociological anthropological researches. McKim Mrriott, Oscar Lewis, Morris Opler, Bernard Cohen, Owen Lynch, and host of Indian scholars R.K. Mukherjee, D.P. Mukherjee, S.C. Dube R.N. Saxena to name just a few have carried out field researches in this part of the country placing it on the National Social Science Atlas.

During the past two decades two significant studies of political life in eastern rural U.P. have been produced by Miriam Sharma (1979) and Masaki Fukunga (1993). Sharma presented her data through a series of case studies of disputes, which illustrate the processes of factional competition and class conflict. Fukunga believes that it is necessary to understand the socio-economic and political forces at the grassroot level to be able to complete the contours of political life at the national level.

What we get from above and many other sporadic publications in eastern UP is that new social, economic and political forces are at work which must be studied in understanding patterns of social change.

The Present Paper

This paper seeks to answer to the issues raised in the beginning of this paper. However, instead forwarding any theory this presents some aspects of relative status of woman in political arena drawing field data from villages of Allahabad district.

The main issue raised in this paper is whether constitutional machinary, i.e., the implementations of the Constitutions (73rd Amendment) Act (1992) is *necessary* and *sufficient* conditions to bring rural women out of their veils to take active part in political life thereby raising their relative status. This issue in fact is the core of the paper.

Our hypothesis in the form of research statements is as follow:

"The independent political decisions are more a feature of the higher castes women than the depressed castes.

(SC and OBC). To create and implement various constitutional devices will do not good altering power structure from men to women"

The Methodology

To test the above hypothesis six villages of Handia Tahsil of Saidabad Block of Allahabad District were selected for intensive field work keeping in view of size of caste wise population. Three types of schedules were constructed, viz., one for. the *General Rural Women*, the other for the *Elected women representatives* of the Panchayat and third for the *elected men of the Panchayat.* These sets were directed to 200 sample (1.68 per cent of the total population) (Table 1 presents the details).

TABLE 1
DISTRIBUTION OF SAMPLE SCHEDULES

Category	*Schedule Sample*	*Percentage*
1. General	72	36
2. OBC	80	40
3. SC	40	20
4. Muslim	08	04
	200	100

Note. Communities represented under (1 are Brahmin and Thakur castes; under (2) Yadav, Maurga, Drobi, Teli, Lohar, Kori, Baniya, Mali, Patel, Nai; under (3) Chamar, Pasi, Mushar, Pal and Harijan, under (4) Backward Community from Muslim constituted minority group.

Discussion and Findings

Due to paucity of space it is not possible here to go in detail analyzing data across variables, viz. age, sex, caste, education, occupation (for detail, see Sinha 2001). Below are noted major findings which are significant in respect of our stated hypothesis.

(1) The constitution of India has granted women equal right of participation in the political process along with equal opportunity and right in education and employment. Articles such as 15, 15 (3), 16(2), 39, 41 through 45 and 326 are particularly important in this respect. On the basis of the recommendation of various committee especially *The National Perspective Plan for Women 1988-200.* Ministory of Human Resource Development, Govt. of India, New Delhi, which recommended a five-point agenda for raising political participation among the women the parliament passed its 73rd Amendment Bill on 22 December 1992. The Act came in force from 24 April 1993. Accordingly the Government of Uttar Pradesh announced the implementation of this Act in 1994. The election were held in U.P. in April 1995. As per provisions laid down in the Act 33 per cent seats in the Panchayat election were reserved for the women in this process; one-third of total seats were also reserved for Scheduled Castes and Scheduled Tribes. The duration of the panchayat was for five years.

(2) Our field investigation reveals that out of total elected women in the area under consideration only 3.7 per cent took part in voting become of their interest in politics; while 44.4 per cent voted in the election at the behest of the male relatives. This power is in the hands of menfolk. 70 per cent of the total elected male respondents were of the opinion that women

should vote only after being advised by the men. How interesting is when 78 per cent elected male respondents replied that women should exercies their franchise?

(3) Lack of interest in politics among the rural women becomes apparents when among elected women only 15 per cent attended Panchayat meeting regularly; about the same percentage of women attended once only while 26 per cent attended irregularly. 44 per cent reported be never attended, our study revealed.

(4) Further, interestingly of all elected women who attended meeting regularly or occasionally only 15 per cent attended by their personal will; 41 per cent attended the meeting escorted by males of their family. This shows rural women are disinterested in local decision making processes.

(5) That the power structure is still in the hands of the men is also evident when we look at compiled data on supervising the activities in the Panchayat office. Thus in 44 per cent cases husbands of the elected members of the Panchayat looked after the offical work; 11 per cent women were guided by their sons; in 4 per cent it was father-in-law who directed the Panchayat activities. (see Tables at the end of the paper).

(6) Nearly 95 per cent elected male respondents held the view that women participated in the election and in fact came in power due to reservation policy; therefore, they merely act as 'Rubber Stamp. About 74 per cent elected respondents felt that their is little change in the social status of women due to Panchayat election and for that matter they do not participate in decision making processes.

(7) A few representatives (less than 5 per cent) are interested in local politics but feel "helpless" because of living in male dominated world. To sum up, why relative status of rural women in North Central India is quite low require a thorough study correlating multiple variables. Our argument is just to

point out that political instruments remain to be ineffective facilitator of social change. Local priviledged group especially the male members control the institution of Panchayat, the foundation of democratic (political) decentralization.

TABLE 2

SHOULD WOMEN PARTICIPATE IN VARIOUS POLITICAL ACTIVITIES?

Category	*Yes*		*No*	
	No. of respondent	*%*	*No. of respondent*	*%*
GC	52	72.2	20	27.7
OBC	44	55	36	45.
SC	29	72.5	11	27.5
Muslim	3	37.5	5	62.5
Total	128	64	72	36

TABLE 3
KNOWLEDGE OF GREAM PRADHAN'S NAME

Category	*Know*		*Do not know*		*Knowledge of Pradhan pati name*	
	No. of respondent	*Percentage*	*No of respondent*	*Percentage*	*No of respondent*	*Percentage*
GC	29	40.3	22	30.6	21	29.2
OBC	16	20.0	34	42.5	30	37.5
SC	.9	22.5	17	42.5	14	35
Muslim	1	12.5	6	7.5	1	12.5
Total	55	27.5	79	39.5	66	33

TABLE 4

KNOWLEDGE ABOUT PANCHAYAT TENURE

Category	*Know*			*Do not know*
	No. of respondent	*Percentage*	*No. of respondent*	*Percentage*
GC	39	54.2	33	45.8
OBC 26	32.5	54	67.5	
	19	1.5	21	52.5
Muslim	2	25	6	75
Total	86	43	114	57

TABLE 5
KNOWLEDGE ABOUT VARIOUS WELFARE PROGRAMMES

	Category	*GC*	*OBC*	*SC*	*Muslim*	*Total*
IRDP	No. of respondents	3	2	1	2	8
	%	4.17	2.5	2.5	25	4
CDP	No. of respondents	4	...	....	...	4
	%	5.56	...	...	...	2
Maternity Benifit Programme	No. of respondents	6	...	4	...	10
	%	8.33	...	10	...	5
Family Welfare Programme	No. of respondents	4	16	...	...	20
	%	5.56	20	...	...	10
Aganbari	No. of respondents	21	21	5	...	47

(Contd.)

(Contd.)

	%	29.2	26.3	12.5	...	23.5
Indra Awas Yojana	No. of respondents	3	47	...	1	51
	%	4.17	58.8	...	12.5	25.5
Kharanjar	No. of respondents	3	48	8	1	60
	%	4.17	60	20	12.5	30
None	No. of respondents	41	32	19	6	98
	%	56.9	40	47.5	75	49
Dwacra	No. of respondents	...	...	...	...	...
	%	...	...	...	...	...
National Family Dev. Programme	No. of respondents	...	...	...	...	...
	%	...	...	...	...	...

References

Fukunga, M., (1993): *Society, Caste and Factional Politics Manmohan, Delhi.*

Rai, Sudha, (1999): Changing Structures of Rural Dominance and Power (Meerut District). Proceedings of a seminar, G.B. Pant Institute of Social Science, Allahabad.

Shah, Ganshyam, (1977): *Social Transformation in India.* Vol.I Rawat, Jaipur.

Sharma, M. (1979) : *The Politics of Inequality.* Hindustan Publication, Delhi.

Sachidanand (1999): Inaugural address of national seminar on Social Change in Uttar Pradesh, G.B. Pant Institute of Social Science, Allahabad.

Sinha, Sageeta, (2001): Political Awareness and Participation of Rural Women of Uttar Pradesh, Unpublished D. Phil Dissertation in Sociology, Allahabad University.

Whyte, Martink, (1978) *The Status of Women in Preindustrial Societies.* Princeton University, France.

15

Literacy and the Status of Rural Women

H.C. Jain

In the form of human resources, almost half of the world population consists of women by ignoring whom, neither any nation, nor world community as a whole can progress. In the words of a thinker, "Humanity cannot survive by being cruel towards women". Still, it is a hard fact that one gets to see discriminatory treatment given to 'the better half' in almost all countries of the world. They have to bear disparities in the fields of education, health, nutrition, and employment, etc. We can well assume the status of the women of the world through the fact among poor illiterates, almost two-third are women. They enjoy 14 per cent of managerial, and administrative, 10 per cent parliamentary and 6 per cent ministerial offices.

World community has been making efforts in the direction of emancipation of women for many decades. Awareness generation toward emancipation of women has been done by United Nations Organisation (UNO) through various meets/conferences, viz. Women's World Conference, (1985) Copenhagen, Women's Meet (1980), Narobi Women's meet of 1985 and Beijing Conference of 1995. Even 1976-85 decade was declared women's decade by UN. Voices were said an this platform towards women's rights. To eradicate all discrimination, U.N. General Assembly made an appeal for positive attitude towards there (women) In fact, we are affective instruments of social change, this needs to be stressed.

Status of a person in society can be measure by two bases: In born and earned values. Among earned values, education is most important which not only emancipates a person but a whole social order. Here, role of literacy in emancipation of rural women has been analysed.

Female Literacy in India

Christiana in his book, *Literacy for Rural Women,* has said that in rural part of Third World, crores of women reside. Wide spread illiteracy among them is a major problem. Among them illiteracy among women above 15 years is like this, Africa—64 per cent, Asia—47.4 per cent, Latin America and Carribean—19.2 per cent and among Arabian Countries, it is 70 per cent. In all under developed countries, 1/4th women on average are literate."

In this, in the beginning of just passed century, female literacy was just 0.6 per cent. Then after independence, in the gone five decades, it enhanced but even today we see wide gap between male and female literacy levels. This gap in the context of rural women literacy can be seen from the table below :

Male-Female Literacy Day in India

Year	*Male per cent*	*Female per cent*	*Common per cent*	*Literacy among Rural Women*
1951	27.16	08.86	18.33	-
1961	40.39	15.33	28.30	10.13
1971	45.95	21.47	34.45	15.52
1981	53.46	28.47	41.43	20.26
1991	64.13	39.29	52.21	30.62
2001	75.08	54.16	65.38	-

It is evident from the above analysis that some improvement is there in female literacy but it is very low in rural women. Illiteracy among SC and ST women of rural area is still widely prevalent.

In India, wide gaps between male-female literacy in rural and township areas is symbol of gender inequalities. Difference between the literacy levels can be well understand from the table below:-

Area and Gender-wise Literacy Rate

Year	*Age*	*Area*	*Total*	*Female*	*Male*	*Gender Inequalities*
1961	5+	Total	28.30	15.33	40.39	25.06
		Rural	22.46	10.13	34.26	24.13
		Urban	54.43	40.46	65.98	25.52
1971	5+	Total	34.45	21.97	45.90	23.98
		Rural	27.89	15.52	39.55	24.03
		Urban	60.22	48.89	69.83	20.99
1981	5+	Total	41.43	28.47	53.46	24.99
		Rural	34.04	20.66	46.73	26.07
		Urban	64.85	54.40	73.92	19.52
1981	7+	Total	43.67	29.88	86.50	26.55
		Rural	36.00	21.70	49.60	27.90
		Urban	67.20	56.30	76.10	20.40
1991	7+	Total	52.21	39.29	64.13	24.84
		Rural	44.69	30.62	57.87	27.25
		Urban	74.08	64.05	81.09	17.04

Source : M.P. Adult Education, p. 251.

It is clear from the above table than the gap between males and females literacy is less in urban as composed to rural side. As per 2001 census survey, total literacy in India is 65.38 per cent. Among this 75.85 is for men and 54.16 for women. It is obvious that almost half of female population is illiterate. Though for the first time, after a decade, there is 14.8 per cent hike in female literacy in urban areas but illiteracy is still a problem among women of backward and weaker section of rural areas.

Female Work Participation and Women

If role of women is analysed from the angle of work participation and economic contribution, in 16 Trillion Dollars economy, women contribute 11 Trillion dollars while they are owners of just 10 per cent income and 1 per cent property Less wages as componed to men and economic exploitation is still common in the world.

If we analyse work participation in India we find that women work participation (F.W.P.) as compared to men in very low as shown in the table below :

Rate of Work Participation in India

Year	*Men*	*Women*
1971	53.81	11.71
1981	53.87	19.08
1991	51.60	22.7

It is clear from the table above that gradually, women work participation is an increase but it is an accepted fact that due to absence of education, much hike in F.W.P. is not possible. In villages, opportunities for valued, useful and employment oriented education in women is not sufficiently given. As per 1971 and 1981 census figures, following is the analysis of female education in rural area.

Percentage of Female Education in Rural Parts

	Educational Leve ls	*1971*	*1981*
1.	Literate	39.66	39.37
2.	Primary	43.92	37.47
3.	Middle	12.32	15.04
4.	Matric	3.47	7.05
5.	Non-Technical	0.28	0.8
6.	Technical	0.28	0.25
7.	Graduation and above	0.27	0.74
	Per cent	100	100

Educational levels of rural women is below urban women in all respects. It is to be mentioned that not even one per cent of women in villages are graduate. Postgraduate, technical, medical, farming, animal husbandry, dairying, teaching related education is completely denied to them. Analysis of this situation as per 1981 census in as below:

Percentage of Female Population as per Education

	Educational Levels	*Rural*	*Urban*
1.	Illiterate	82.04	52.18
2.	Just Literate	7.07	12.39
3.	Primary	6.73	14.15
4.	Middle	2.70	9.08
5.	Matriculate	1.27	9.23
6.	Non-technical Education	0.01	0.06
7.	Technical Education	0.04	0.16
8.	Graduate	0.13	2.75
9.	Graduate (non-Technical)	-	1.84
10.	Post Graduate (non-Technical)	-	0.51
11.	Graduate (Technical and above)	-	0.40
12.	Engineering and Technology	-	0.01
13.	Medical	-	0.07
14.	Farming, Animal Husbandry	-	0.00
15.	Teaching	-	0.32
16.	Others	-	-
	Total	247553652	130803766

Source : Census India, 1981, Series 1 Part-II.

Both in urban and rural society relation of a man in close to his profession. An educated man can perform any work better than an uneducated man. In the words of Pt. Jawahar Lal Nehru: "To awaken people, we shall first have to awaken women with development of women, family, village and the nation will develop." Women will get opportunities for overall development and participation when they are given education without any prejudices and gender disparities.

Social Development and Literacy

There are some parameters for social development and values in the context of which importance of education and literacy can be understood. World Development Report, 1983 presents some relationship between percentage of literacy and same indicators like birth rate, mortality rate, infant mortality rate and contraceptive used by women in South Asean countries. There is positive relation between literacy and quality of life. This can be seen as below:

Social Development and Literacy Rate

Country	Literacy 1980	Birth Rate Per Thousand 1981	Death Rate Per Thousand 1981	Infant Mortality Rate (0-1) 1981	Calories intake per head 1981	Life Duration 1981	Contraception By women
India	36	35	13	121	1880	52	23
Pakistan	24	46	16	123	2184	50	6
Nepal	19	44	20	148	1977	45	4
Bangladesh	26	47	18	135	1960	48	12
Sri Lanka	85	27	6	43	2238	69	41

Source : World Development Report—1983.

This is evident from the above table that in Sri Lanka, education level is better, so are other indicators which means that education is directly related to the quality of life. Gunnar Mirdal has expressed the same facts in these words, "Literacy opens the ways to communication which otherwise remain closed. This is a prime necessity from the angle of skill and wisdom."

Apart from law literacy rates of rural women of India, poverty mal-nutrition, sub standard life style and high productivity rates also contribute to their low social status. All these factors somehow get affected with education and literacy. World Family Health Survey Report, 1992 found 38 per cent household women below the age of 15 yrs. which certifies child marriage in the country. Birth rate of 1991-92 was 28.7 per cent while 57 per cent were illiterate. In other words, one women on average produces 3.7 children but in cities this is 2.7 per cent among illiterate women, it is 4 and among high school pass women, it is 2.2. Among Muslim women, this rate is 4.4. Similarly, average gap between two children was 2.7 yrs., i.e. 32 months whole among 8 born children each is born after 18 months. Evidently, mode spread illiteracy keeps women away from family welfare awareness. Note only birth rate, but mortality rate also gets affected with illiteracy. As is evident from table below :

Mother Education and Child and Infant Mortality Rate

(1992-93, per Thousand)

Education	*Infant-Mortality Rate*	*Child Mortality Rate*
Illiterate	100.6	44.3
Literate	62.5	22.8
Middle School	56.1	9.2
High School	37.1	6.2

Source : National Family Health Survey, 1992-93.

Among women, malnutrition is responsible for bad health and anaemia which affects their work output. Due to malnutrition high mother mortality rate is found in Indian Apart from this. As per world match, 53 per cent babies in India are under weight due to women's malnutrition.

In rural parts, social condition of women are analysed in relation with education. Child marriage, dawry widow remarriage etc. affect then in a negative way. Flesh trade and prostitution is also due to illiteracy only.

Government of India celebrated year 2001 as Women's Empowerment year. Objective of the same is to help women develop in all spheres of life.

STEP for employment, Training-cum Employment programme for women, SHG and Empowerment Projects etc. main women's emancipation programmes being implemented by Government of India. But the dream will come true only after rural women are given due attention.

References

1. Christiana, C., *Literacy for Rural Women,* UNESCO, 1991.

2. Jain, H.C., Mahila Vikas the Ayaam M.P. Bharat Gyan Vigyan Samiti, Bhopal, 1993.

3. Garg, Bhwani Shanker, Gender, Equality and Educational Environment, National Adult Education union, New Delhi.

4. Bhandare, Murlidhor C. (from Hindi Version).

5. Report—National Family Health (from Hindi Version).

6. IAEA (Hindi Version).

7. Selected Socio-economic Statistics of India, 1999 **(Hindi Version)**.

16
Social Status of Women

Badri Prasad

In the words of Charles Farrier, French thinker, "Social, Political and Economic status of women is the Indicator of Civilisation of a Nation."

Fate of women is depicted in poem of Raghuvir Sahai like this,

"पढ़िये गीता, बनिये सीता
फिर इन सबमें तू लगा पलीता
किसी मूर्ख की बन परिपीता
निज घरबार बसाईये
होय कंटीली आंखे गीली
लकड़ी गीली तबियत ढीली
भरकर भात पकाईये" ।।

> "Read Gita, become Sita and then bow to all these evils, became wife of a fool, start new home, shed tears, met fuel wood, sickness, still keep on cooking. This is the fate of a women"

To this, one can add that 'herself sleep hungry'. Status of women can also be understand by this folk song of U.P. (translated in English).

"The day a daughter was born to my brother, women is assassinated with gold knife. The day I was born to my mother, she looked for the 'Khurpi' and destroyed it."

There is no need for deep investigation of academic level to understand the status of women in society. This can be noticed from which happens around us everyday. Be it the list of activities done by man and woman, opportunities for education to both, opportunities for progress at profession, opportunities for entertainment and promotion of happier, social rules, limits towards both men and women, one can well see double standards indicating disparities of men and women, provided one wants to see. Those who are interested in the status quo, not only that they do not want to see it, instead they defend it through religion, social limits, customs, traditions, and culture, etc. Due to this what about an ordinary persons, even policy makers, politicians and even intellectuals tend to neglect this aspect. Even if a women's day, a meeting or a workshop is organised, it does not go beyond formalities.

In India and whole world, sexual image of a women is found for which some so-called idioms are famous, viz.

It is good to batter as much as possible a woman, a dog and wall nut tree

> Heaven is at the feet of husband.
>
> Nodles is not rice, women is not life.
>
> "Marrying a women is like buying a donkey which I can ride or bast I wish."
>
> Daughters and cows can be taken anywhere.
>
> (On consolation of a dead wife to husband) on breakage of a utensil cover, a new one can be bought.
>
> On death of a daughter, debt is waived off, it first gives some pain but ultimately great relief.

All these literatures, says and sayings are expressions of widespread belief in society.

Religion has played an important role in pushing women to

lower status and then keeping there.

According to leading economist Amarta Sen, "where their is inequality, people are not able so see it and in other walks of life also, they victims of inequalities. It has mode deep roots and denied section has accepted it as their fate. So the inequalities are getting deeper. So it becomes it more difficult to condemn this situation. There are disparities in the family it is really very difficult to see. Ignorance about deep inequalities, is an one May, symbolic of the fact that they are very deep and on the other hand, it becomes a cause for continuity of these inequalities. Since beginning there is a difference between position of males and females and the status of each is different. Each religion has taught women to remain below men and formed such principles. Here is a look at different religions:-

> A women should dependant on father, husband and son in childhood, youth and oldage respectively.
>
> Husband may be wicked, values or even made, he is a God to his wife:
>
> Killing of drunkard, untouchable and women are minor crimes.
>
> 'Rigveda' has said women to be psychologically weak, luring and leading to hell.
>
> According to *Mahabharata*, qualities of a woman and falsehood, non-thinking, folly and excessive greed, cruelty,
>
> Tulsi Das in *Ramayana* says that drawn, illiterate, untouchable and animal, all are to be beaten.

Quran Sharif clearly says that a man has right over a woman because God has made him above woman and he invests in keeping a woman so, woman should follow man. If she disobeys, it is the right of man to rebuke, beat and punish her and if need be, divorce her.

Christianity was brought by women, so this is considered more progressive religion. Bible says that a woman should bow before man the way one does before God. Husband is the owner of his wife. Wife is under husband the way church is under Christ.

We get such examples in religions but religions are standing on popular faith, a sensitive and emotional subject it is. Logical analysis on public level is not possible resulting in exploitation and unjustifiable treatment meted out to women.

Role of Education in Continued Inequalities of Women

Our educational books play important role in keeping women at low level. On one side, constitution is taught aiming at establishment of an egalitarian society. Articles 12-34 talk of fundamental rights that consider all equal irrespective of caste, religion, language, etc. Articles 14, 15 16 talk of equal participation of woman in development. These articles talk of equal opportunities for employment under law. One side, there is a Chapter teaching all this as it is, on the other side, there are numerous books lowering significance of women. NCERT books are maintaining the status quo. Here is one example of 300 syllabus books:

1. In 181 stories, men in the centre only in 9 women.
2. 263 pictures of men and 75 of women.
3. In life characters chapters, 78 on men, 3 on women.
4. All chapters proving women inactive.
5. 113 works of economic important by men and 11 by women. Men are shown performing all acts and women only nursing, maids, teachers, queen, princess, etc.
6. Names of 50 per cent female characters missing, introduced as daughter, daughter-in-law, mother, grand mother, maid, etc.
7. A father mourning at the birth of daughter.

In the survey of Ms. K. Nishchal, such list is very long. This is enough to prove what outlook of children is being developed through education one can also drive from the fact that 6.5 per cent work, 10 per cent income, 1 per cent property and 60 per cent illiteracy goes to almost 50 per cent women of the world. Modern development has also contributed to this Vandana Shiva calls it patriarchic set up.

- More of modern machinery, technology and industry is available to men and women world in old manual way. Work previously performed by women have been given to men after mechanisation.
- Training for new methods of agriculture, new technology is provided to men reducing continuously work participation of women.
- Decreasing participation of poor rural women in development process day by day.

Some facts on this are below :-

1. Insecure and insufficient employment lack of resources for irrigation, irregular fields work cause lack of labour for women that too on less wages than men irrespective of constitutional provisions.
2. Distribution of work based on disparities leads to denial of certain works to women.
3. Performing household work alongwith labour is a compulsion for women. Much labour, unbalanced diet, repeated pregnancies, lack of medical treatment make life of women quite miserable.
4. Lack of health facilities lead to weakness and inaccessibility of the same adds to the problem.
5. Absence of labour laws in unorganised sector leading to no leave, work during pregnancy, lack to work immediately after delivery are troublesome for women. Villages of Bankheri block, Hoshangabad district present this picture very clearly.
6. They have to undergo sexual exploitation by contractors.

landlords, moneyed people, and government officials. Work of women has not got proper place in Governmental surveys also which affects national policy-making and bad conditions of women continue 'Bonded Labour in India' by Mahsweta Devi and Nirmala Ghosh is story of female exploitation in rural society.

Almost are Calta families of Babu and bonded labourers, Kamla alias Daulti was from Dhoura village whose father borrowed 1200 to buy grains for the wedding of his eldest daughter.

When Daulti was of 16, a Brahmin of her village had offered to repay his whole debt provided he hands Daulti over to him saying that he wants to marry Daulti.

To keep in mind, women here are very beautiful and a local saying that initial 10 years of youth of women are full of merry making and then starts tear shedding.

Father of Daulti agreed, his debt was repaid but Daulti was taken for prostitution to Meerut. She worked in flesh trade for two years and that man took all her income as repayment of debt. She became a bonded labourer. After she reached thirty and started losing beauty, her rate reduced. Brahmin brought her to her country village for prostitution in the village itself.

After Brahmin's death, his son took over the responsibility. He constructed a small hut for her to continue work.

Daulti did not know if she had repaid her debt in twenty years 'work' or not. She is still alive, carries on with the 'work' and gives money to her owner.

Rajasthan Government had started a project called. 'Sathin' for walfare and awakening of women. Beginning of the project on initiative of Anil Brotha went well. Voluntary organisation of Rajasthan trained Sathins. Then Chief Minister, showing commitment to the cause had said that words of 'Shathins' are his words, orders.

In the beginning, there were positive results but then feudal influence, social evils and the opponents stepped in. 'Sathini' would struggle for equal wages to women, stop child marriage and death feasts, prepare women to speak their hert and organised them against exploitation. Then government and employees of Rajasthan started checking 'Sathins' work. They had been struggling as trade unions for long time. Voluntary organisations, women activists and National Commission for Women tried their best but of no use. Story of Sathin Bhanwri Devi is known to all.

In an unequal set up, equal distribution also leads to inequalities. Report of CIDA says, "Aid to third world nations benefitted men more and less women while this was not the objective of the aid." The same thing has been said in NPP for women, 1998.

Ranowned writer and social worker Mahasweta Devi says that "men of each section of society controls women for which our social order is responsible. A man born in this set-up is bound to exploit women. This difference will continue unless class-difference are removed.

If the whole set up remains like this, status of women will obviously continued to be low. Inequality in any walk of life cannot be removed separately. Women may be strengthened economically and educationally, unless and until each sphere of life is changed, basic differences in status of women cannot be removed.

17
Status of Women in Tribal Society

Sri Nath Sharma

In the book *Story of Dumbs* Smt. Meneka Gandhi writes, "Have you even thought, had there be no animals, what would had of our life been. Many plants will disappear without butterflies. Similarly, right from...., to bear and dear etc. all animals are like security shield of mankind."[1] But this is so tragic that our intellect attracts us towards animals but less bothered about the fact what will happen when tribals dependant on these animals and their culture will elope, then what will happen. What will happen when the tribal women—pivot of natural and human balance, shall disappear.

Women Liberation movement of today show that so called intellectual nations talk of human rights of women but tribal woman is not discussed at all. Be it Cairo conference of 1994 on Population and Development[2] or Encyclopaedia of Indian Women by Anuradha Sharma.[3] This state causes worry but neither humanists nor sociologists, nor voluntary organisations are worried about this aspect. Megha Patekar and some NGOs associated with Sardar Sarovar movements are doing this work.

In preface of the book, *Hum Savita,* Ila Bhatt writes that "When women started to be recognised as a human being, it was felt that she is the slave of slave. In all environments, cultures, social orders, war and peace, everywhere women was attacked exploited and tortured and this gave birth to her freedom movement."[4] She also raised a question, "Where has the liberation movement reached? How far is yet to go?" Only answer to this is that still there is no change in basic relations. Raj Kishore writes, "Women is the last colony of man"[5] Humanist Leila Dubey, "in the so-called modern society, women has no right over her children because she is the earth and the peasant to sow is the man, the one who sows shall reap."[6] These sociologists are against exploitation of women.[7] But the question is still a question in the lack of action.

Whatever may be the speed of development after 1947, development of tribals is still under question. Policies of disolation and assimilation have not been much fruitful. Even if me ignore major problems of tribal women, no efforts have been made to resolve their minor problems either. Mastram Kapoor writes "Life of Bharmor and Gaddi women is full of hardwork. In winters, they go to plains with children loaded in their backs where they face many problems... some difficulties of Himachal women are clear and inevitable like hills. No government has done anything for them. Even today they are struggling for water, food, toilets, negetables, fuels, etc."[8]

Woman is more painful than groups facing prolonged deprivation. Same is true of tribal women of Singrauli Tehsil, Siddhi District, M.P. which are discussing in the present paper. of Siddhi district M.P. touches Varanasi and Allahabad districts of U.P. People displaced by coal mines live in different parts of Singrauli Tehsil. Problems of these displaced families have reached the peak.

Baiga, Khairwar and Gaur tribes of around Singrauli Tehsil are living in various villages of Singrauli under rehabilitation plans. Their living standard is still very low despite many administrative efforts. Under a plan, 26 SHGs of tribal women are being formed. This state in the past 3 years is as below:

- Project is being run by Institute of Regional Analysis, Bhopal.
- One women social scientist each is working from Dudhichua, Jayant and Nighahi.
- SHGs set up in all 26 villages.
- These SHGs provide training in sports, education, adult female education, gardening and forestry.
- One woman members of IRA deposits money in the bank on the basis of financial achievements of each group.[8]

Efforts for the awakening of tribal women by NGOs at the directions of social scientists are admirable. This too appears so at ground level only. During an informal interview with these tribal women, it was found that money received through SHG's cannot be spent at their wishes". Some times, this amount is snatched by their husband on the way to home.

They are contented with educational efforts and like discussions. But they are bound to follow men. Marxian faith that 'economic independence leads to social liberation' can be true here.[9]

On the basis of difference of tribes and tribal studies, it can be said that status of women is different in different tribes. Thus, fact of any one tribe cannot be generalised.

Tribal women are not tender. They work equal to men in farms, for animals and in forests. Among some tribes, character of women is not determined by her virginity. Cultural values convey male-female equality in certain tribes as sadd for P. Prakash[10] for Nicobar tribes. But this cannot be denied that both economic and traditional factors affect the status of equality of tribal women.

References

1. Gandhi Meneka, *Story of Dumbs,* Pustak Mahal, Delhi, 1997 Introduction.

2. International Conference on Population and Development, Family Planning Association of India, Mumbai, 1994.

3. Sharma, Anuradha, *Encyclopaedia of India Women,* Commonwealth Publishers, New Delhi, 1998, Vol. I.

4. Bhatt, Ila, *Hum Savita,* Ansuya Trust, Bhopal, 1994.

5. Dubey, Leila, *Dharti Aur Beej,* (ed. Rajkishore), pp. 50-56.

6. Dubey, Shyamcharan, *Sociology of Development*, Vani Prakashan, New Delhi 1994, pp. 23-24

7. Kapoor, Mastram, *Sam Samayik Pratikriyayen,* Samta Prakashan, New Delhi, 1996, p. 98.

8. Vishwas, P.C., *Santhal of the Santhal Parganas*, Indian Scheduled Tribes Services Union, Delhi, 1956, p. 8.

9. Prakash, P., *The Role Women Among Car Nicobars,* Vanya Jati, 1958 Vol. 6.

18
Tribal Women Yesterday, Today and Tomorrow

Dr. Anil Jain • Dr. S.K. Tripathi

"If you want developments you will have to emancipate women, society will develop automatically with the development of women".

—*Jawahar Lal Nehru*

Indian Constitution recognised equality of rights of men and women but without question, admits disparities in spheres of roles and actions of women. After this constitutional equality, position of women has legally strengthened but in practice, even today, they are victims of exploitations and atrocities. Status of women in developing society can be analysed as below :-

It is important to understand social structure before evaluating the position of women. Social norms, social values system affects social aspiration of both men and women and determines the role and status of women in society. Among these institution, the most important heritage system give moral basis to family and relations, marriage and perceptions towards religious beliefs. Ideal parameters do not change on that speed on which industrial and educational development, cash system, growing population, changeable prices and changes in standards of living. They are evident from such cracks.

Thinking Towards Women

Manu has determined double standard policy towards women.

In words, he signifies the worship of woman and principle laid down is,

पिता रक्षति कौमार्य, भर्न्ता रक्षति यौवने
पुत्रों रक्षति वार्धक्ये न स्त्री स्वातंत्रता मर्हति

"Meaning that father protects childhood, husband protects youth, son protects in oldage, a women is never free."

Hinduism has provided secondary and disrespecting position to women. Her prime duty is to serve father, husband and son in childhood, youth and oldage respectively.

Religion like Buddhism, Jainism, Vir, Shaiv, and Sikhism tried to bring improvement in the status of women. But they too considered women as mother or wife only. She got the place below men in society.

Quran Sharif in Islam give equal status to men and women and do not consider women obstacles in the way to religion. Still interpretation of different 'Aayats' of Quran over time gave low status women which convey cultural values of that time. Women cannot become Mulla, Imam read, Namaz in Mosque, religious organisation and interfere with legal matters. Seclusion became the social symbol.

In Christianity, women can take part in religious celebrations, but they are not given the organisational responsibility. Bible presents women as luring, misguiding and thus gives the right to property (of women) to her husband.

Pairs religious give place to honour to women in society and family. Women are entitled to keep property, gain religious education and all allowed to divorce and remarry. But a men is allowed to marry a non-Parsi while a women is not.

Among Kawaylis, women plays her role in activities of religious rituals in family and group but does not take part in worship of tribal Gods. She cannot even play role in community discipline and public morality teachings.

Thus, all religions give second grade status to women.

Middle contributed the most to the deterioration in the status of women. Situation worsened with Mughal invasions, women got convicted inside the houses. Her education was stapped. Social evils like child marriage, uneven marriages, Sati, restriction on widow remarriage, etc. made them almost animals. Child marriage and Sati contributed to the maximum.

From where started treatment to women and low mentality towards them. Here male can say that if power means moral power, i.e., tolerance, then definitely women is more powerful than man.

Women Today

Their work is now gone beyond family responsibilities to make them self-dependent. Educated women support in various arrangements—the husband and family members. They have become Prime Minister, diplomats, freedom fighters and even officials to UNO.

Today, she is again moving towards equality. By law, she enjoys equality with men but is also herself party to removal of social disparities. Sense of equality is getting strong in women. They have started stepping in social, political, technical, administrative and religious fields and also society is becoming liber towards them. They have started winning prerogatives in certain industries and professions like nursing, textile and fashion designing, telephone operating and typing, etc. and thus proven false the saying like "only men are capable."

One can see new change in all age, income and social groups of women starting from the age of 'Satya' and 'Suvaran'', crossing freedom struggle age of Sarojini Naidu, Aruna Asaf Ali, educators and doctors of 5th, 6th decade, now in 22nd century, they have became engineers, pilots, all India services employees, sculptor, journalist, female Judge, etc. Her achievements are touching height of sky.

Women Tomorrow

Women of 21st century finds herself capable in every sphere. Changed social set up. Changing political picture is going to take women very high. Today, they have progressed a lot. Be her Bichendri Pal, Kiran Bedi, Arundhati Roy, Medha Patekar or Mayawati, they are living examples of female emancipation. Their future seems to be better than men. Today in each sphere, they are ahead by men. Day is not far when they will overshadow men in all spheres.

References

1. *Human Rights and Women Atrocities*, Sudharani Srivastava and Ragini Srivastava, Common Wealth Publishers, New Delhi, 2001.

2. *Parivartan,* Manoj Kumar Singh, Aditya Publishers, *Beena 2000 Bharat me Samajik.*

3. *Mahila Vikas Karyakram,* Dr. Asha Rani, Inashri Publishers, Jaipur, 1997.

4. *Mahila Vikas Ki Nayi Dishayen,* Pushpa Motyani, Karnawati Publishers, Ahmedabad, 1998.

5. *Mahila Shramik-Samajik* Sthiti Arey. Samasyayen, Dr. Jasmine Lawrence, Aditya Publishers, Beena, 1999.

6. *Samaj Kalyan Nari Deeksha Sanskriti,* Dr. Jai Sh. S. Bhatt, Aditya Publishers, Beena, 1998.

Recommendations

1. Increased participation of women in the conservation and management of natural resources namely joint forest management, common property rights such as grasing grounds, water bodies and pestures.

2. Larger participation of women in water management.

3. Women should be given better opportunities to play an effective role in family dispute-management such as cases related to dowry, bride price, divorce, maintenance of widows and divorced women and of children. It is proposed to constitute family tribunals consisting of women members for proper family disputes management.

4. Women should be empowered economically, educationally and politically at a faster speed.

   (i) Economic empowerment can be achieved by giving them the right to inherit parental or deceased husband's or divorced husband's property.

   (ii) There is a need to create an increasing awareness about educational empowerment. Efforts should be made to introduce and encourage distance education to the potential school/college going girls who are deprived of educational facilities due to non - accessibility of an educational institutions.

   (iii) For political empowerment the provision for 33 per cent reservation for women in Assembly and Parliament would go along way in improving their over all status.

5. Women should actively involved in the struggle movements against ecological disbalance and environmental pollution, etc.

6. Universities and other higher places of learning should make special efforts in providing need-based research projects to

women scholars and for this purpose a higher financial allocation should be made.

7. National Commission for Women should be made more powerful by giving them judicial powers including power to summon the guilty.

Signatories

1. Prof. S.K. Gupta (New Delhi)
2. Prof. A.R.N. Srivastava (Allahabad)
3. Prof. A.N. Sandhwar (Ranchi)
4. Prof. A.P. Singh (Srinagar, Garhwal)
5. Prof. Ramesh Chaube (Sagar)
6. Dr. B.R. Rizvi (Udaipur)
7. Dr. Kalpana Saini (Sagar)